# DARWIN
## COLLEGE

*A 50th Anniversary Portrait*

Edited by **Elisabeth Leedham-Green**
and **Catharine Walston**

THIRD MILLENNIUM
PUBLISHING. LONDON

**Darwin College: A 50th Anniversary Portrait**

2013 © Darwin College and Third Millennium Publishing Limited
First published in 2013 by Third Millennium Publishing Limited,
a subsidiary of Third Millennium Information Limited,
2–5 Benjamin Street, London, United Kingdom, EC1M 5QL

**www.tmiltd.com**

**ISBN 978 1 906507 93 0**

*British Library Cataloguing in Publication Data.* A CIP catalogue record
for this book is available from the British Library.

Edited by Catharine Walston
Designed by Matthew Wilson
Production by Bonnie Murray
Reprographics by Studio Fasoli, Verona, Italy
Printing by Printer Trento, Italy

# CONTENTS

# Foreword by the Master

Fifty years is a long time, yet not so very long: a working lifetime, yet mere moments in the eight centuries of the University. It's a fine time to look back, to remember the basis on which we go forwards.

Darwin has grown organically. It wasn't born in a single giant conception, jumping fully grown out of the forehead of the University like Athena from Zeus, but rather from the musing and friendship of four College Bursars. Since then we've been lucky enough to grow slowly, in a Darwinian way, from so simple a beginning. Over time, endless forms most beautiful and most wonderful are being evolved. After 50 years, I hope we're today still in the deep Archaean aeon of our College's evolution – now wait another 750 years to see what we can do!

Colleges are unusual institutions. They're living communities, always changing. That means they develop memory. A tall tree may be busy photosynthesising, providing nesting habitat for birds, and shading a student reading a book. But to do this the tree needs roots and a trunk that have grown over many years, finding water and keeping the tree upright. The roots of the College are now deep, and the trunk tall.

Darwin College has become a very special place in Cambridge, with its lovely river frontage and quiet Study Centre counterbalanced by the busy Dining Hall and very popular if rather noisy bar. Today we are one

of Cambridge's larger colleges. All this has been able to evolve because, to change metaphors, the foundations of the College were so well laid 50 years ago, and the buildings since have been good, designed carefully to fit in and add to the original homes, with materials that don't attempt to take over. The fine buildings are the least of our riches – Darwin is an extraordinary inter-generational community, among the world's brightest points on the intellectual map.

But it hasn't changed. There's still that cheerfulness and friendly informality about the place that has been here since the beginning, and which is important in allowing members to succeed. Whether it's spending long, long hours on some recalcitrant analytical instrument, or struggling over an obscure text in a dead language, Darwinians don't do extraordinary things because they are trying to be extraordinary – but simply because the puzzles are there and deserve to be studied.

As a college, Darwin is extraordinarily fortunate to be formed on the basis of the Darwin family home, and we are most grateful for the generosity of the Darwin family and their strong support for us. Ever since Professor (Sir) George Darwin purchased Newnham Grange as his family home, this has been a place to think and enquire. My great-grandparents lived just across Queen's Road in Newnham Cottage, and my grandfather, R.H. Fowler, worked very closely and was good friends with Sir Charles Darwin, George's son. Thus, as children, my father and his siblings knew the Darwin home quite well: indeed, just before we were married, my husband-to-be was taken round the College by my aunt and told much amusing gossip, which he has judiciously forgotten. My father and siblings could almost claim to be among the first Darwin students, for in the late 1920s some went to school in the Malting House, now part of our College. Teaching methods were somewhat unorthodox – my very young father seems to have spent most of his time with a bunsen burner! His school report approvingly describes a pyromaniac, while an aunt recalls gardening and dissection. The school's founder, the extraordinary Geoffrey Pyke, had advertised in *Nature* for a teacher, so it's not surprising that science was encouraged.

My own arrival at the College was – it feels only yesterday – just over 40 years ago. Darwin seemed a very

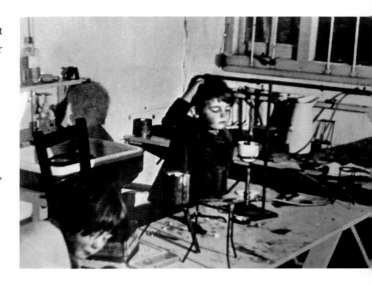

***Above:*** *Peter Fowler in the Malting House, 1927.*

***Below:*** *Mary Fowler on an OBS ship, 1975.*

**Right:** *Mary Fowler, centre, 1973.*

**Opposite:** *The Punt House.*

exotic place to me, a shy 22-year-old having seen little more than the inside of a maths lecture theatre, and not knowing anything much at all about the earth sciences prior to starting my PhD in the Department of Geodesy and Geophysics. This was a college of people who walked barefoot across Greenland or quoted Gladstone on Homer's wine-dark sea. I was rapidly shipped off to a research ship in the eastern Mediterranean, and then, on my return, ordered to write a 'News and Views' for *Nature* about a completely different area, the Philippine Sea. Nowadays all that seems extraordinary – both health and safety, and the intense competition to get into *Nature* prohibit!

And so it went: it has often been said that youth is far too precious to be spent by the inexperienced young,

and we hardly appreciated the delights. Marriage came (with the reception in the Darwin Dining Hall) – same college, both earth scientists, members of the same church – and I found myself, in very short order, having appendicitis, emerging from Addenbrooke's to stagger down the aisle wary of my appendix scar, bouncing around the North Atlantic launching the ocean-bottom seismometers overboard, and then travelling out to Zimbabwe for the real honeymoon (fieldwork on Archaean lavas and stromatolites).

Science then, in the troubled economy of the 1970s, had not much money. I recall one problem: we didn't know the orientation of the seismometers when they landed on the ocean floor some three kilometres down. Spending substantial amounts on equipment to work at those depths was impossible, so I simply poured boiling hot jelly ('jell-o' to North Americans) into a cylinder containing an exposed compass needle. When it set on the sea floor, the direction was recorded. As has often been said of British science, we hadn't got the money, so we had to think! As students we were enormously privileged back then: not financially (an allotment of vegetables had a key role in the household budget for our growing family), but to be permitted the openness of mind and the freedom of curiosity that so distinguished Charles Darwin. And I hope now too, that freedom, the search for truth in nature and in life, still remains and will long continue as the informal, friendly spirit of Darwin College.

*Mary Fowler*

# THE COLLEGE CAMPUS

### Roger France

### THE MAIN SITE

Looking around the verdant setting of Darwin College today it needs a leap of imagination to visualise the area as it was in the early 19th century: an industrial part of Cambridge, set about by mills, warehouses, a brewery and a rubbish dump. To the east were the King's and Bishop's Mills; to the south was the Granta Brewery, a malting house and Newnham Mill. What we now call 'the Backs' had been a strip of flat land prone to flooding from the western branch of the Cam. For many years the Corporation dumped the town's waste here to raise the level of the ground. Westwards, fields reached as far as Newnham Road allowing easy access for the delivery of milk and meat from local farms.

Water has been an ever-present neighbour; several rivulets converge here. This was the last navigable part of the Cam for boats carrying goods from King's Lynn. The site of the present-day Study Centre was originally an island between two branches of the river, each with its own bridge. Logically, this area was called 'Small Bridges', and Richard Harraden's view of 1798 shows the last remaining of these, with Queens' College beyond.

In the Middle Ages tolls were levied on those who crossed bridges, a job usually done by hermits or priests. For this purpose a small building was erected somewhere here, its existence being recalled in the name now given to that part of Darwin College called 'the Hermitage' (previously 'the Armitage').

The story of the older buildings on the main campus site is one that is intimately connected with the lives and fortunes of several Cambridge citizens – traders, teachers and members of the professions – who bought land in this soggy area west of the Cam and who developed it into the substantial built quarter of the city that the College now represents.

**Above:** *Harraden's view of Queens' College (1798) showing one of the old bridges with the Beales' granary on the extreme left.*

**Opposite:** *The Old Granary.*

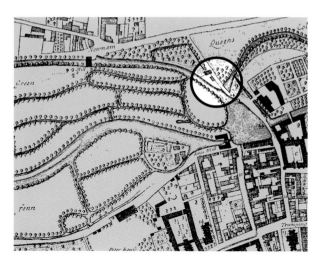

*Detail from Loggan's map of 1688 showing the two branches of the river and the first dwelling on the site.*

*Sketch by Gwen Raverat of Newnham Grange from Silver Street, 1890s, showing a later kitchen extension.*

Historically, the main College site is an elongated triangle of land bounded by Silver Street and Newnham Road, with the third side inscribed by the curve of the river. Occupation of this waterlogged area started at the end of the Civil War – some three centuries before the founding of the College – when Richard Dickenson built a house beside the western bridge. David Loggan's map of 1688 shows this butting slightly into the causeway.

### THE OLDER BUILDINGS

In the 1790s the leases on the land were taken over by Patrick Beales, who built up a family business trading in corn and coal. He and his successors ran businesses here for the best part of a century, and the way in which they disposed of parts of their landholdings helps to explain the idiosyncrasies of the College campus.

Beales was responsible for building the riverside granary. He replaced Dickenson's house with a residence that we now know as Newnham Grange. In the Corporation's records it is described as a 'substantial mansion', being a double-fronted, two-storey house in the Georgian style with a parapet gutter and plentiful

cellarage. The late 19th-century ensemble is shown in Gwen Raverat's sketch.

Although the designer is not known, it is a house in the Georgian tradition, certainly solidly built, and displaying decorative details fashionable at the time: fireplace surrounds show Adamesque imagery and ceiling mouldings contain acanthus-like leaf motifs in the plasterwork. In an auction catalogue it was described as 'a most excellent Brick-built family residence … one of the best built houses in the Town'. The name 'Newnham Grange' was given to it by Sir George Darwin when he bought it in 1884. It is this house that, in 1963, Sir George's descendants agreed should form the nucleus for a new college bearing the family name. Today, this building forms the heart of the College: the present 'Old Library' has been created by demolishing two partition walls that bounded the original entrance corridor; the Bursar is rumoured to inhabit Sir George's former study, while the Master's office is in a former bedroom. Its domestic character remains.

The Old Granary was a key part of the Beales' trading business, its waterfront location allowing the loading and unloading of goods from boats. (It is shown on the extreme left of Harraden's print.) It had substantial storage space and many of the original Baltic pine beams remain today. However, as the fortunes of the corn and coal trade declined, the building became empty. It was Sir George Darwin who later reshaped this part of the site. He demolished some parts of the Old Granary to create a tennis court, and he converted others into living accommodation for his family. For these changes he appointed a London architect, J.J. Stevenson, a designer in the Arts and Crafts tradition. It was he who was responsible for the oriel window and quaint balconies that now adorn the riverside. It was not an easy conversion into a residence; the combination of a curving plan with differing floor levels is the cause of the awkward room shapes which are now the main feature of the Old Granary building. A feature of particular art historical interest that remains here is the 'Painted Room' accessible along the raised riverside gallery that used to look over the tennis court.

Two islands faced the site which Sir George had bought, a unique bonus for a riverside residence. He leased them from the Corporation and then had two bridges built to save his family from ferrying across the river. Nowadays the smaller island, nearest to Newnham Grange, is owned outright by the College, but the larger is still leased from the local authority.

Sir George asked a London engineer, F.H. Anson, to design the bridge which would connect his mansion to the smaller island. It may have been intended as an echo of Queens' 'Mathematical' bridge, but its span is shorter and its design is simpler. Regrettably the foundations were found to be unstable in the 1990s, so the whole bridge had to be reconstructed on firmer footings. This has resulted in a complete rebuild to approximately the same design as the original, a task achieved by the generosity of Hugh and Julia Fleming.

*Members of the Darwin family on the balcony of the Old Granary.*

## LATER CAMPUS BUILDINGS

During the century in which the Beales family had an interest in the site several changes took place reflecting the family's changing fortunes in the face of shifts in the local economy. Bit by bit parts were sold off, allowing the construction of the Hermitage and Newnham Terrace.

### The Hermitage

The first plot to be developed in 1853, immediately to the west of the Grange, was by Swann Hurrell, another Cambridge businessman and brother-in-law to Patrick Beales. He built a villa in the Regency style – somewhat conservative for the time – constructed with local grey gault brick. Its principal feature is the large bow window that faces the river. The Hermitage owes its name to Stephen Parkinson, a mathematics tutor at St John's College who resided there from 1864. He instigated several changes and it is probably he who added the less elegant three-storey extension abutting Newnham Road. He built a new staircase and had his initials and those of his wife carved in the lower newel post. Although its neo-classical porch has vanished, much of its original gracious character is in evidence in the Parlour and first-floor Entertaining Room, now the Richard King Room. Parkinson's widow,

*The Painted Room. Members of the Darwin family painted recognisable portraits of various significant members of the University onto the walls, where there are also versions of* The Visitation *and* The Baptism *by Gwen Raverat and her husband, Jacques, painted in the summer of 1914.*

Elizabeth, left the building to St John's College. In turn, St John's allowed the fledgling New Hall to use the premises as its first home and, when New Hall decamped to Huntingdon Road, sold them to Darwin College.

*The Dining Hall designed by Bill Howell.*

## Newnham Terrace

Another subdivision of the original site was the construction of Newnham Terrace. It was built during the 1850s and is typical of mid-Victorian townhouse developments, providing spacious family houses which could also accommodate students and servants. Over time several of these buildings came into the ownership of King's College. Subsequently Darwin College has been able to buy them at different times and convert them into accommodation for graduate members. At No.1 Newnham Terrace an extra seminar room and other facilities have been incorporated. After 50 years of development the only part of the original triangular site that does not belong to the College is the Granta pub. A particular asset of the terrace is the series of gardens which stretch down to the river. The decision to retain most of the original garden walls adds to the small-scale domestic character of this part of the campus.

## Malting House

Always on the lookout for student accommodation near to the main campus, an advertisement for the sale of the Malting House in Newnham Road gave the College its chance to expand again.

There is evidence that the building had been another part of the Beales family's commercial activities as they tried to gain a foothold in the brewing industry, for in the 1830s their business had been described as 'maltsters and brewers'. However, this did not last. A brewery had existed over the road at what is now the Granta pub. The building had originally been used as a warehouse and oast house as well, but when its use as a malting house ceased the eastern part was converted into a residence occupied by the Dean of Trinity College, Dr Stewart. In 1924 it became the 'Malting House School', a forerunner of the children's 'community schools'. The structure of the Malting House is typical of a late 18th- or early 19th-century industrial building, but on changing to residential use in 1909 its east end had to be rebuilt to accommodate road widening. The architects appointed were Smith and Brewer, designers in the Arts and Crafts tradition. Some delightful contemporary details remain today inside, including numerous glazed tiles and a magnificent early electric chandelier over the staircase.

The College won a competitive tender for the purchase of the Malting House in 2003 and graduate members moved in later that year. An additional 14 bed-sitting rooms had now been provided. The original oast house makes an impressive seminar or common room, the only such environment for scholarly pursuit in the University.

## TWENTIETH-CENTURY BUILDINGS

While Darwin was still on its way to becoming a fully-fledged college in Cambridge it was clear that there would be need for a new dining hall, increased office space and more on-site accommodation for graduate members. A new building to link Newnham Grange and the Hermitage was the obvious solution. The firm of Howell, Killick, Partridge and Amis was approached late in 1963. It was a newly established architectural practice which had recently been appointed to design the University's Graduate Centre in Granta Place. Bill Howell became the lead partner for Darwin College.

The design of the Dining Hall follows that of the main refectory at the Graduate Centre: a pyramidal lantern atop a sloping roof, with a decidedly prominent

*The Malting House seen from the east.*

*The Dining Hall
from the gardens.*

support system. Chamfered corners were a feature of the firm's designs in their attempt to break away from the 'tyranny of the rectangle'.

The building which links the Grange to the Hermitage was also by Howell. It was named the Rayne Building in recognition of the generous benefaction from the Rayne Foundation for the construction of both it and the Dining Hall. In design terms the linking building is a conscious attempt to create an urban terrace with its neighbours. When seen from Silver Street Bridge or Queen's Road the Rayne Building's 20th-century personality does not vie with its earlier neighbours. Rather, it complements them in scale, texture and materials.

Although an architect in the modernist tradition, Howell paid careful attention to the interiors of the older buildings. Sets of 19th-century furniture were sought for the Parlour in the Hermitage, and many inherited features of the Grange were kept. This showed a sensitivity to inherited buildings that was rare for its time.

### The Newnham Grange extension

The next addition to the campus was an eastern wing to Newnham Grange. This was designed by David Roberts and Geoffrey Clarke in 1976 and completed three years later.

Although the extension impinged onto a lawn another ten rooms were added for graduate members as well as some administrative offices. The residential rooms all have balconies with views out towards the Old Granary and the Mill Pond, and the building aligns effortlessly with the Grange. Roberts served as a member of the University's Department of Architecture for many years and had designed several new buildings locally. The new extension building was awarded a Civic Design commendation in 1980.

### The Study Centre

With dining and on-site accommodation achieved the College now looked to provide a library and study centre. A limited competition was launched. There was serious debate about the best location, for the site is severely

*The north front of the Rayne Building showing the way in which the architects attempted to create an urban terrace in conjunction with the neighbouring buildings.*

The College wanted a building that would act as a place where graduate members could sit and study in a space outside the confines of their bed-sitting rooms and where proper computing facilities could be housed. In thinking about this project the architects had visited several college libraries and had noted the traditional use of wood in their interiors. A design emerged in which the scale of the interior was broken down into five low-level computer rooms separated by staircases. These, in turn, led to a series of high-level study bays with views out over Laundress Green. The architects wanted the interior to read as one continuous piece of furniture, so both desks and structure were designed in oak, this material continuing onto the south elevation.

Initially the design was found unacceptable to the local authority, partly because the building would sever the unique stretch of landscape between the Backs to the north and the meadows to the south. On appeal, however, the need for College study space prevailed and today Darwinians can enjoy one of the finest riverside settings in which to create their texts. The Study Centre was awarded an RIBA design award in 1994.

constrained. Ultimately, a building was chosen on the former kitchen garden east of the Old Granary. The winning firm was Dixon Jones, London architects who were engaged in reshaping the Royal Opera House in Covent Garden at the time.

*The Study Centre seen from the south.*

## OTHER SITES

Darwin College has always been on the lookout for opportunities to house graduate members near the main campus. Usefully, an opportunity arose in 1993 after prolonged negotiations, for the College to buy a plot of land belonging to Newnham College in Wordsworth Grove. The firm of Dixon Jones was appointed again and their design produced accommodation for 28 graduate members. The setting was that of Edwardian and late Victorian houses in Wordsworth Grove and in particular that of Basil Champneys' magnificent buildings for Newnham College built between 1874 and 1913.

The new building was named Frank Young House in honour of Darwin's first Master. In terms of material and scale the front that faces Wordsworth Grove reflects the context of this Victorian suburb, while the elevation facing south is more distinctively modern. It is a three-sided courtyard with cascading roofs looking out over playing

*Frank Young House from across the playing fields. It can be seen circled on the maps above and above right.*

18

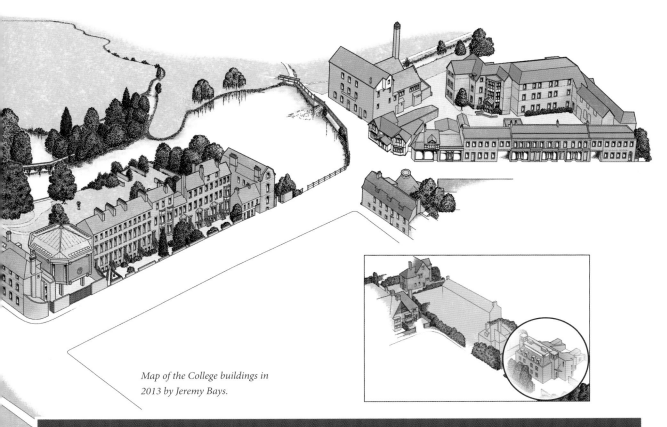

*Map of the College buildings in 2013 by Jeremy Bays.*

## MATRIMONIAL CELEBRATIONS AT DARWIN COLLEGE

The almost pastoral riverside aspects of the garden of Darwin College, combined with the splendid Dining Hall accessed from the garden by the 'flying steps', makes the College a very special location for a wedding reception.

My Fellowship at Darwin gave me and my family the privilege of celebrating the wedding of our oldest daughter, Lucy, in the College. A reception was held involving pre-meal drinks (with string quartet) in the games room, a seated three-course wedding breakfast in the Hall with the traditional speeches and toasts, followed by an informal gathering in the garden. The event was arranged with the help of the Bursar (Peter Brindle), the catering manager (Ian MacTulloch-Gair) and the wine steward (Karalyn Patterson). Family members decorated the dining tables with a stunning display of arranged flowers which transformed the Hall from its usual formal lines into a display of joyful

informality, fit for matrimonial celebrations. The Butler, Andy Evans, ensured the smooth running of the catering, including the cutting and distribution of the wedding cake.

*Dr Tony Cox*

fields. An echo of the rooftop balustrading of Champneys' nearby buildings has been attempted at high-level with a balcony set between two large-scale staircase lanterns. Complete with kitchens and common rooms the building offers a peaceful location for graduate members to live in a small and distinctive community close to the main campus.

The last modern building to be added to the College's estate is Gwen Raverat House. It is tucked inconspicuously off Newnham Road in Anderson's Court behind Newnham Mill (now a restaurant). It is in an awkwardly shaped site, sandwiched between a remnant of old industrial Cambridge and the original settlement of Newnham. It was designed by a local firm of architects, Lyster Grillet and Harding, originally for the Kelsey Housing Association, and intended for King's College, but Darwin was able to purchase it in 1996 and it came to house 54 graduate members.

Elsewhere the College has been able to purchase several properties as they have come onto the market. These have usually been the Victorian or Edwardian residences that exist in Barton Road and Wordsworth Grove, and there are 'flats' at King's Road and Ashworth

Park. Proximity to the main campus has always been an important consideration.

### An intriguing estate

On reaching 50 years of age Darwin College has amassed a fascinating collection of buildings, mostly on one site. It boasts one of the longest collegiate riverfronts – and certainly the most romantic – and it is unique in having two private islands.

The College has inherited a stock of the city's 18th-century industrial buildings and 19th-century townhouses, and it has added some distinguished, award-winning 20th-century additions. It is domestic rather than institutional in character, a feature that must appeal to members who come from one of many countries around the world to study here. The Old Granary, the Grange, the Hermitage and the Malting House are all listed as being of special architectural or historic interest and therefore officially 'heritage assets' for the community at large. In this respect each type of building has its own needs for long-term conservation.

## BECOMING ONE OF THE TWELVE APOSTLES

Although my Cambridge life began at Trinity in September 1965, it can be said to have started flourishing two months later when my supervisor, Gerd Buchdahl, who had just been made a Fellow of Darwin, asked me in the enthusiastic manner that characterised him: 'How would you like to be one of the 12 apostles?' 'Isn't it a bit late?' I replied. He retorted in a suitably professorial tone of voice that 12 was the number of students that the Fellows wanted to recruit from the 'old' colleges to launch a graduate one, which would aspire to be 'not only different but better'. I found the apostolic approach amusing from a man who had turned to philosophy, as he told his students, because he was interested in 'big questions' and mainly whether there were any valid philosophical arguments for the existence of God. Fascinated by the great religious traditions, but academically aloof, Gerd used his extensive knowledge of the Bible as a source of suitable quotations or, as in this case, of startling metaphors.

I was reluctant to leave my room in New Court at Trinity but as soon as I saw the Old Granary I knew that life on the river was the one for me. I took up residence in January 1966 and was soon greeted by two surprises. The first was that I ran the risk of waking up one morning in the river. I had only been at Darwin for a couple of weeks when the Bursar called on me early one morning to say that a young engineer had been summoned to check whether the foundations of the Old Granary were really stable. He was not a Cambridge graduate, but a thorough-going modern engineer for whom ancient buildings were suspect of decrepitude.

I accompanied him to the river and he poked around. After a few minutes he declared in the most dramatic way that he would not sleep in a building that was in danger of sliding into the river. The reaction of the Bursar illustrates the optimism that, I trust, is still a trait of the Darwinian, man or woman. 'Let's wait until it slides!' I must confess, however, that before going to bed that night I examined my pillow to see whether it would float. The second surprise came a few days later when someone rapped on my door. Upon opening I found an elderly lady (everyone over 60 was old for me at the time … I have revised my views since) who bustled in saying, 'Sorry to bother you but I just had to see this room once again. Bertie and I often had tea on the balcony.' The only Bertie I knew at the time was Bertie Wooster, the creation of P.G. Wodehouse, but there was no doubt that her Bertie was not fictional. It soon transpired that she meant Bertrand Russell, and I was regaled with a lively description of what went on during tea at the Old Granary.

*William Shea*

*Gerd Buchdahl.*

# THE SITE AND GARDENS

## OUR COLLEGE'S RIVER SETTING

**Peter Friend**

A changing climate has been a key contributing factor in providing our College with its attractive setting, and will continue to play a significant role in the future!

In common with most of eastern Britain, the landscapes around Cambridge owe their arrangement of slopes, hills and rivers to episodes that occurred during the Ice Age. It has recently been discovered that this Ice Age extended for millions of years and consisted of many tens of episodes when the climate changed from times of intense cold to times when it was distinctly warmer than at present.

Our Cambridge area was completely covered by an ice sheet during only one of these episodes. About 450,000 years ago ice extended from the north as far as north London, covering Cambridgeshire with an ice sheet some 100 metres thick. Later this ice sheet melted and Cambridgeshire emerged, variably covered with the pebbles, sand and mud that the ice had carried with it. It was at this time that the River Cam first became an identifiable feature, and it has never ceased to exist since then. It did, however, move to occupy different courses across many tens of kilometres of Cambridgeshire, and at different levels, as further changes of climate modified the behaviour of the river and the surrounding landscapes.

The Cam, as we now know it, has probably occupied roughly its present course for several thousands of years, flowing northwards past present-day Darwin College and along the Backs towards Castle Hill, which is underlain by a resistant tongue of chalk where a shallow ford became the river crossing, the first site of a Cam-bridge, and now the site of Magdalene Bridge.

The appearance of the Cam floodplain just upstream from Darwin is marked by two river channels, clearly embanked and modified by man, and the watermill history around the Newnham millpool and the foundations of the former King's Mill (beside The Mill pub) make the origin of these features clear. Other natural channels also drain Lammas Land, however, and it is intriguing to think that these may date from much earlier times, when a different climate regime caused the River Cam to flood more violently at times of heavier snow melt, producing channels and islands of sand and mud, that may have first built the Little and Big Islands we are able to enjoy today.

More extreme river-flooding is being forecast, and we are aware that flood river levels in the Cambridge area are strongly controlled by the engineering works that determine flood levels across the whole Fenland basin. In Darwin we shall increasingly depend on this support to help us to continue to enjoy our setting.

## THE GARDEN

### Derek Bendall

With Newnham Grange the nascent College inherited a family home of great character. It has defined the physical nature of the College as more homely and welcoming than the imposing buildings of traditional colleges might appear, especially to overseas students. By comparison with the buildings of older colleges the house is modest – the garden, by contrast, is as interesting as any to be found in other colleges.

By and large the College garden has not been planned but has grown organically in a way determined by the site, its history and a concept of the role of the garden in the life of the College. Above all there is the river, which is the hero of the story, to use the expression of Margaret Keynes in *A House by the River*. The Old Granary and the curious roadside wall of the croquet lawn owe their existence to the wharves and granaries that occupied this part of the riverbank.

The garden of Newnham Grange as we know it was largely the work of J.J. Stevenson, the architect employed by George Darwin when he purchased the property. Unlike some modern architects he seems to have had a feeling not only for the building he was concerned with (Newnham Grange) but also its immediate surroundings, seeing the site as a whole. Stevenson demolished most of the granaries, and in the space freed by their removal he created a tennis lawn. By the time Darwin College was founded this had become known as the croquet lawn, perhaps reflecting the ageing of the previous occupants of

**N ↑**

Study Centre
(kitchen garden)

Old Granary

Roberts extension

Newnham Grange

Silver Street

Rayne Building

Croquet lawn

Little Island

Pl

Pa

CB

Lammas Land

P

j  W  A

Newnham Terrace

1
2
3
4
9
10
11
12

Herbaceous

Roses

Woodland

Fruit and vegetables

Big Island

Newnham Road

**Key**

A     Armillary sundial
CB    Copper beech
J     Jurassic garden
P     Pear
Pa    Parrotia
Pl    Oriental plane
W     Wollemi pine

*Above:* Garden map.

*Right:* The croquet lawn.

## THE LAST PIECE

Here is Darwin College on the corner of Silver Street and Newnham Terrace, with the small arm of the river Cam running between the main grounds and the island. The multi-coloured lines, in the blocks depicting the College buildings, represent all the people who have been and will be members of Darwin College, people varied and colourful in their own ways, which is how I remember the Darwin people when I was there. The blue lines in the blocks depicting the river represent all that has flowed by Darwin and all that will flow by, bringing changes and things new. The green lines in the block depicting the island represent the growth and development of Darwin College over the years, and on into the future. And the two-part block in the top centre represents the putting into place of the last piece of the puzzle: the acquisition of No.4 Newnham Terrace. The title comes from this last piece, and makes an allusion to *Period Piece* by Gwen Raverat, who spent her childhood in Newnham Grange: the house that formed the first piece of Darwin College. She also became an artist noted for her distinctive style of line drawings and woodcuts.

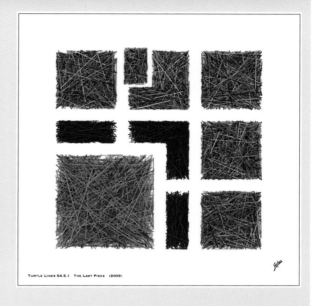

TURTLE LINES S4.5.1 THE LAST PIECE (2009)

The Last Piece *by Afriko (Dr Tim Smithers, 1977–81). A computational painting in Turtle Lines style created for Darwin College to mark the acquisition of No.4 Newnham Terrace. Programmed using ACSLogo developed by Alan Smith and running under OS10.5 on an Apple MacBook Pro.*

the house. By retaining the riverside wall of one granary he made a picturesque gallery overlooking the tennis court. Out of the one remaining granary, at the east end of the site, together with the attached Counting House which faced the road, he created an eccentric house which came to be occupied by several distinguished tenants, and eventually by Gwen Raverat in her last years.

The character of the garden, as the College first knew it, was thus largely the work of Stevenson, except for two subsequent innovations by George Darwin. Beyond the Old Granary there was a narrow strip of land leading up to Silver Street Bridge, with the river on one side and the road on the other. George Darwin turned this into a kitchen garden. On the riverbank he erected a wire trellis on which he espaliered fruit trees – apples, pears and quince. When the Study Centre was built upon the old kitchen garden cuttings were taken from the quince and planted against the roadside wall of the croquet lawn, alongside fruit trees that were already there. Secondly, as we shall see, there was the question of how one reached the two islands, because at the time of Stevenson's work there were no bridges.

On the town side of the house, when the College acquired it in 1964, there was the croquet lawn, the Old Granary and the kitchen garden. On the other side, the garden door (now the connecting door between Newnham Grange and the Rayne Building) led onto a lawn, which was dominated by the magnificent copper

*The walkway to the Big Island.*

beech tree by the river, the focal point of the whole garden. When this was planted is unknown, but it was already a sizeable tree when Gwen Raverat was a child, and she climbed it to make a tree house. By now it must be nearly 200 years old and is sadly reaching the end of its life. The heart of that massive trunk is rotten and, although this is common with ancient trees, ultrasound scanning has shown that the rot is spreading, generating fears that the trunk would soon become unable to support the great weight of the branches. Members of the College recently returned from Easter break to find the tree greatly diminished in size, particularly by removal of the great branch overhanging the river which was a threat to punters passing underneath. The tree is, in fact, more resilient than at first appeared, when it looked as if it was about to be felled entirely. It is now rebelling against this brutal treatment and putting out fresh new branches, so we may be able to enjoy it as a centrepiece of the garden for a few more years yet.

The oriental plane on the Little Island (as well, probably, as the three planes on the Big Island) is probably of similar age to the beech, judging by estimates of the age of the great plane in the Fellows' Garden at Emmanuel College and the known age of the tree in Jesus College (planted 1802). The tall pear tree outside the Hall is also venerable, but its true age is unknown. It stands in what was previously the Hermitage garden and according to Margaret Keynes was planted by the Beales. Each year it still provides a magnificent display of blossom as a marker of spring. It is not a good eating pear and in any case the fruit when it comes is now out of reach.

One more feature of the garden as we know it today already existed when the Darwins moved into Newnham Grange, and that is the two islands. The islands add an extra dimension to the garden, providing space and solitude. Birds as well as humans can appreciate the peace of the Big Island, and some nesting boxes were recently installed to encourage them. The Little Island has provided a useful space where parties might be held, close to but separate from the main College buildings, and it has proved particularly popular for holding barbecues. This is a rare, if not unique feature amongst College gardens, but the Darwin garden is one to be used. It is an informal English garden, not even *un jardin anglais* or a formally informal garden according to the French or German stereotype of an English garden. Some durable but unobtrusive hard-

2 / The Site and Gardens

The ownership of the islands is curious, emphasised perhaps by the fact that they are in the parish of Little St Mary's, whereas Newnham Grange is in St Botolph's. Historically the islands, along with the strip of land that became the Darwins' kitchen garden, were owned by the Borough and were leased to George Darwin. Behind the two islands lay an area of Lammas Land, which also used to be an island, but seems to be so no longer. This was owned by the Fosters who ran the King's Mill (demolished in 1927) at the end of Mill Lane. George Darwin extended his estate by buying this Lammas Land as pasturage for horses. Eventually, when it ceased to be of any practical value, Sir Charles Darwin, George and Maud's successor at Newnham Grange, effected a deal with the Borough whereby the latter gained the freehold of Lammas Land in exchange for freehold of the Little Island and the kitchen garden site, which passed to Sir Charles. So the College now owns the Little Island but has a long lease on the Big Island.

At first the Darwins would have needed to ferry across to the islands, and the character they have now

standing was laid on the island a few years ago following a design of Dominic Milner, an architecture student, who used various kinds of reclaimed brick and hardwood slats.

**Above:** *Suicide Sunday on the Little Island, 2013.*

**Right:** *Bridge design to link the Big Island to Newnham Terrace Gardens by Julian Hakes, who studied for a DipArch at Darwin from 1995–7 before completing his MPhil in 1998. Since then, in partnership with his wife, he has designed bridges all over the world, most notably in Moscow, Boston and Bristol. He was also the winner of the Drapers Award for Best Footwear Designer of the Year 2012 for his innovative 'Mojito' shoe design, which has no foot plate.*

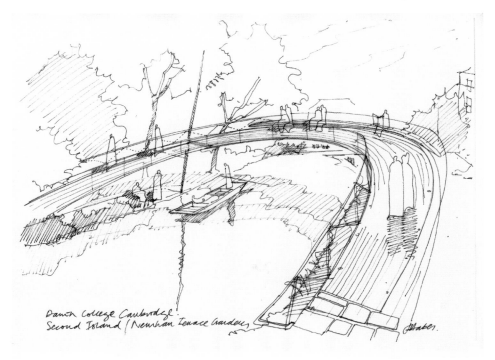

Darwin College Cambridge.
Second Island / Newnham Terrace Gardens

has been determined to a considerable extent by the two bridges that George Darwin built. He linked the Little Island to the mainland by a wooden bridge that in the mind of Darwinians has achieved almost the iconic status that is associated with the bridge in Monet's garden at Giverny. It was geographically impossible for the Big Island to be linked directly to Darwin-owned mainland, so a causeway bridge was designed to connect one island to the other. The Big Island is thus not quite so easily accessible, which helps to give it that air of privacy. There has been talk recently, now that we own all the river bank opposite the Big Island, of a third bridge to provide a direct link, but that is a question for the future.

When the College was founded in 1964, the first addition to the Newnham Grange property came with the purchase of the Hermitage from St John's College when New Hall (now Murray Edwards College) moved to its new buildings at the top of Castle Hill. This provided a welcome addition to the Darwin garden when the dividing wall was demolished, which was offset by the irresistible opportunities it offered for further building. It was always clear that even with the acquisition of the Hermitage the College would require further buildings for a Dining Hall and student accommodation. This became possible

remarkably quickly with a generous donation from the Rayne Foundation, and so the College became established on a firm physical basis with erection of the Rayne Building linking Newnham Grange with the Hermitage, and the Hall filling a space between the Hermitage and Newnham Terrace. As it turns out, of course, even this range of buildings has proved inadequate. The eastwards extension of Newnham Grange by David Roberts provided needed accommodation but it encroached on the croquet lawn, changing its proportions. The wooden balconies on the end wall provide the occupants of the rooms with fresh air and a cool place to sit and talk on a summer evening. There is a formality about the design which has been emphasised in a satisfying way by planting clipped yews at the base of the wall.

With the completion of the Roberts extension in the early 1970s the garden seemed adequate for the size of the College as it then was, and it entered a 20-year period of static maintenance, but even so it became increasingly inadequate along with the accommodation, as the College continued to grow. The College had always had ambitions to reestablish the original Beales estate by acquiring Newnham Terrace. Most of it was owned by King's College and used as student accommodation, but there were two

*Darwin Backs, five panels painted by Carol Williams, one of Darwin College Boat Club's early successes who rowed in the Blue boat in 1972.*

28

notable exceptions. King's had its own plans for developing student accommodation and in 1985 Darwin was able to buy Nos 2 and 3, but direct access from the main site was blocked by the private ownership of No.1. Eventually in 1992 No.1 was bought from the estate of Mrs Gooderson, the rather blatant ambition of the College to break through the south wall of the Hall, as marked in its brickwork, could be realised, and the garden acquired welcome new space by spreading into the back gardens of 1, 2 and 3. The first step, therefore, was to demolish the walls at the rear of Nos 1 and 2, and the wall between the Hermitage site and No.1 was truncated. A topographical error was committed when a stone marking the boundary between the parishes of St Botolph's and Little St Mary's was moved into the end of this shortened wall, the true boundary being the river. These demolitions were not welcomed by everyone, as some felt the opportunity should be taken to develop different small, relatively enclosed gardens in the Sissinghurst manner. However, with the purchase of the remaining King's houses (9–12; note that 5–8 have never existed) in 2000 and No.4 in 2010 from the Ely Diocese, it became possible to realise both types: the open space as lawn as well as a series of smaller enclosed gardens. So 1992 was the beginning of an exciting period of development in the garden which is fortunately guided by the knowledge and experience of Arkley Nurseries, and by the imaginative approach adopted by Rod Ailes and Ros Keep and latterly also by Andrew Birkett.

Proceeding southwards through the garden, starting at the north end of the croquet lawn, we come first of all to a small bed under the wall of the Roberts extension. This has been planted as a dry garden, a xerophytic garden planted mostly with cacti, some of which have to be lifted for the winter, so the planting tends to vary a little from one year to the next. If we turn to the left the bridge, recently rebuilt with the help of a generous donation from Hugh and Julia Fleming following George Darwin's design, takes us over to the Little Island, where we may note in passing one of the more unusual plants on the Little Island, which is a *Parrotia*, or Persian Ironwood

*The de-crowned copper beech during the winter of 2012–13.*

tree. This is in the witch-hazel family and like witch-hazel (*Hamamelis*) itself, which is a bush with yellow flowers, it blooms in late winter when the tree is bare of leaves, but its flowers are a deep red colour, and it has the added attraction that its leaves become fringed with the red hue of anthocyanin before they fall in the autumn.

Turning back to the main garden we pass under the pergola that is outside what was George Darwin's study (now the Bursar's office), which is still draped with his vine (which gives only small, black grapes but, being pre-phyloxera, was used to propogate new vines for French vineyards) and a luxuriant fig. Continuing a little further we might come to a sudden halt and turning back realise that we have been assailed by the scent of *Daphne odora*, which will not be the only time that we discover scented plants in the garden. Moving on we come to the main lawn, with the copper beech and the river opposite Lammas Land on our left. Under the shade of the beech, where little else would grow, a semicircle of *Sarcococca* was planted in the early days of the College. *Sarcococca* is dull in summer, but it is evergreen and produces flowers in winter that give a

*Graduate members practising tai chi in front of the armillary sundial.*

heady scent. Now that the beech has been so drastically pruned the site is more open and we may have lost the beech within not very many years. Then we can think afresh about how to treat this key position in the garden.

The focal point of the enlarged lawn is the armillary sundial presented by Joyce Graham, who played a key part in the life of the College as Master's secretary over many years. As we approach it we should notice first the small area of ground behind the old pear tree and backing onto the wall of No.1 Newnham Terrace. This has been treated for acid-loving plants. The outstanding plant here is the sweet gum tree, or liquidambar (*Liquidambar styriciflua*), which has been planted particularly because of the brilliant flame colour the leaves acquire in autumn before they fall, a welcoming feature as the new academic year begins. Following the rhythm of the year the emphasis of the garden is to provide colour in autumn, winter and

spring, leaving the summer to look after itself. Passing round the wall we come to what the gardener likes to call the Jurassic garden, not entirely accurately perhaps, but in evolutionary terms the plants here predate the development of the angiosperms (mainly a Cretaceous phenomenon). The garden is announced by the recent planting of a Wollemi pine (*Wollemia nobilis*) donated by three retiring Research Fellows with Antipodean connections, Ellen Nisbet, Giselle Walker and Camilla Hinde. This is an extraordinary tree, probably genuinely Jurassic judging by fossil evidence, but thought to be extinct until a grove of wild trees was discovered in 1994 in a gorge of the Wollemi National Park, not far from Sydney in Australia. It is closely related to the monkey puzzle tree (*Araucaria*). In Jurassic times it may have been spread quite widely over the southern continent of Gondwana but seems to have survived, in small numbers, in only one or two isolated and restricted sites in Australia. Over the past few years there has been a campaign to encourage people around the world to plant seedlings or cuttings in order to preserve it. Having admired this tree we pass into a small walled courtyard behind No.1. This is a sheltered area with damp soil planted with ferns and with strong statements by a Chusan palm (*Trachycarpus fortunei*) and a tree fern, *Dicksonia*, which again is probably a genuinely Jurassic plant. At the moment the centre of the courtyard is marked out by a baby date palm.

Continuing our walk through the main garden we come to the newest area of the garden behind No.4 and the remaining houses of Newnham Terrace. This is gradually being developed, as time and resources become available. The overriding principle here was to retain most of the small, distinct spaces defined by the garden walls of the houses, removing only small sections of the walls to provide direct access all the way through to the end of the terrace. First we come to No.4; herbaceous borders have been established here against the walls. This is a traditionally English feature, but the planting here emphasises strong colours, such as the yellows of Rudbeckia and Michaelmas daisies, that with luck will persist into October, when the College is at its busiest. It also provides a relatively quiet and secluded area where people can relax on the riverbank. Next we come to a rose garden, the inspiration of Torsten Krude and designed by Andrew Birkett in such a way that all the roses are accessible in a series of small triangular beds provided with 'smelling stones'. There is also some mixed planting, including even a young eucalypt. The third area is only now, in 2013, being developed. It contains a pair of puzzling trees, which Rod Ailes has identified as quince rootstocks which have been allowed to grow up from pear trees which have died. The intention is to make a woodland garden out of this space. Finally we come to a little orchard with two old apple trees still fruiting well. A plum tree and a mulberry have been planted here, and against the sunny wall some enthusiastic graduate members have established a small vegetable garden. In the corner by the river there is a magnificent old yew tree.

These individual spaces add much to the variety of the garden as a whole. The trees and walls are fixed, but the planting scheme otherwise could change from time to time. They emphasise the variety of ways in which the garden is used by all members of the College. The lawn holds it all together, and is not only an interesting space in itself, but is now large enough for the May Ball and summer parties, and is used every sunny day by people continuing conversations started over lunch in the Hall. Those wishing to spend the afternoon quietly working on their dissertation with a laptop can retire to the Big Island, as wi-fi covers the whole garden. The background to all this is a rich, often colourful botanical variety, designed to inform, and perhaps also to pose questions. Why, for example, do the leaves of some trees turn red in October before they fall, and others turn yellow or brown?

Having reached the end of our walk through the garden we can see potential for further development in various ways, and in particular the hero of the story needs a little more space to be seen as deserved. One day it might be possible to walk all along the riverbank behind Newnham Terrace.

## THE DARWIN ALLOTMENT
### Charlotte Rae

In January 2011, the College gave a group of enthusiastic, if less than knowledgeable, graduate members permission to strip an overgrown patch of shrubs in the end garden of No.12 Newnham Terrace, in order to start cultivating our own vegetable patch.

On the first of several murky February Sunday afternoons, we spent hours clearing the woody shrubs to construct beds of fertile soil. However, our efforts were soon hampered, when in the process of digging over the exposed ground, several bones made their way to the surface. Optimism was high that we had made the discovery of a lifetime and found bones belonging to hobbits. The College, however, was concerned by the possibility that the bones could be human remains. Torsten Krude, the gardens' Fellow, arranged for Adrian Friday at the Department of Zoology to analyse the bones. To our disappointment, the bones did not belong to hobbits, nor were they human, which did at least mean that we could continue preparing for planting, rather than calling in the archaeologists and police. Adrian's

*Clearing the allotment plot of shrubs, February 2011.*

*Success in the first summer, July 2011.*

*The punt filled with compost and ready for planting.*

expert analysis revealed our collection to contain 'the astragalus of a cow, the bottom and top ends of the humerus of a sheep, and a trunk vertebra of a large breed of dog'. The dog we assumed to be a pet lovingly buried, while the cow and sheep we had to accept were probably leftovers from a stew.

Soil improved, spring on its way, we got planting. Requests from our Antipodean allotment members to grow aubergines, mangoes and bananas were unrealistic, but we sowed seeds for runner and French beans, tomatoes, carrots, courgettes, potatoes, beetroot, lettuce and herbs. Much to our surprise, almost everything did well.

In the summer of 2011, one of Darwin's punt fleet sprang a leak. The computer officer Espen and Admiral of the Punts, Ed Oughton, came to the conclusion that the leaking punt would make a superb vegetable planter at the allotment. Transport of the one-tonne punt from the river to dry land, and along Newnham Terrace, posed a significant problem but, eventually, 20 students turned out to haul the punt from the water, carry it through the Darwin gardens, and safely deposit *Iguana* in her new home. Since her installation, she has helped to grow a large crop of spinach, fought off a caterpillar infestation on the radishes, and recently produced our first harvest of garlic.

The second year of the allotment's operation, 2012, was unfortunately less bountiful than the first. Encouraged by our beginner's luck, we expanded the range of crops to include broad beans, rainbow chard, pumpkins and spinach. The spinach was the only crop to perform really well, what with the dreadful weather resulting in disaster: the tomatoes were at least a month behind in development, and by the time they formed fruit in September, were already being damaged by night frosts. The runner beans – the one crop the international members of the allotment were assured could not fail – pretty much failed, with only a few beans developing very late in the season.

Still, in hopes of better weather, and undeterred by previous failures, we are expanding our range to include parsnips, leeks and garlic. The ever-increasing range of allotment crops is influenced in part by the allotment's new director, Teodora Boneva, who takes a more 'experimental' approach to vegetable gardening than my British preference for regimented kitchen garden rows with not a weed in sight. Although we differ on the details of plot tidiness, it's delightful to know that, come the summer, the Darwin allotment will continue to boast canes of beans, potatoes sprouting from mounds of soil, and pumpkins trailing across the grass.

## ANIMAL BEHAVIOUR

Undoubtedly Darwin's most famous ethologist, or animal behaviourist, is Dian Fossey, whose murder at her gorilla research station in Rwanda in 1985 has ensured she remains a controversial figure. She gained her PhD in 1974 based on her work with gorillas in the Virunga National Park. Among those who came to study with her was Kelly Stewart, one of the twin daughters of actor James Stewart, who was also awarded her PhD at Darwin in 1974. She has built a career as a primatologist and is a research associate at the University of California, Davis.

Another Darwinian concerned with animal conservation is Rob Malpas (1975–9), CEO and founder of the Conservation Development Centre in Nairobi, which offers strategic advice to governments and NGOs on natural resource conservation in relation to human development. His area of expertise is African elephants, and he has over 30 years' experience in East Africa, where he ran the International Union for Conservation of Nature (IUCN) regional office for more than a decade.

Patricia Moehlman has also made a career in animal behaviour in East Africa:

'I was a member of Darwin College in 1980/1 when I was a visiting scientist at the Sub-Department of Animal Behaviour in Madingley. I spent most of the year working on golden jackal (*Canis aureus*) and silver-backed jackal (*Canis mesomelas*) data from the Serengeti, Tanzania. During the year I co-authored a chapter on cooperation, altruism and restraint in the reproduction of carnivores for Patrick Bateson's *Perspectives in Ethology*. I also went to the Galapagos to do a few months' research on feral asses on Volcano Alcedo.

After the year in Cambridge, I was on faculty of the Yale School of Forestry and Environmental Sciences for five years. Then I was a senior conservation scientist for the Wildlife Conservation Society for ten years. In 1989, I started doing research and conservation on the critically endangered African wild ass (ancestor of the domestic donkey) in Somalia, Ethiopia and Eritrea. That work

*Above: Dian Fossey.*

*Below: Golden jackal pair and pups, taken by Patricia Moehlman.*

continues to the present and involves spending time in extreme deserts and working with extraordinary people. In 1997, I was appointed Chair of the IUCN/SSC Equid Specialist Group, and this has allowed me to assist in the research and conservation of endangered equids in non-African places like Turkmenistan and Mongolia.

The research and conservation work on jackals is now in its 40th year. Their behavioral ecology continues to fascinate me and I learn something new each day in the field. The research has expanded to include the evolution of cooperative breeding in family *Canidae*.

The time spent at Darwin College and Cambridge University expanded my horizons and led to valued, long-term friendships. I have been extremely fortunate to have great teachers and wonderful colleagues throughout this journey of exploration of wild places and ideas.'

## MAY BALL MEMOIRS

The first day that the Darwin College Students Association (DCSA) committee assembled in 1973 we had to decide whether to organise a May Ball, which apparently was the top challenge for any student association at Cambridge. The experience had been that previous Darwin May Balls – at least the last one – had failed, with heavy financial losses; the main reason for this, we learned later, had been that Darwin's May Ball actually took place in May. To organise a May Ball was not an easy task, particularly since we faced strong competition from other colleges with more experience and resources; for size reasons, we would not be able to compete with big budgets for rock bands and orchestras, among other features.

The May Ball Committee was formed and for months worked normally, everyone doing a fantastic job. Darwin's May Ball posters presented a romantic couple, a photo I took of Chris Todd, an American law student, and Jane, his visiting girlfriend, on Darwin's bridge. Lisa Keller, an American history student, was in charge of printing the poster in grey tones on pastel-coloured paper, so we covered Cambridge with our image of an intimate and romantic May Ball. As the date drew near we faced the challenge of hiring good bands on a limited budget, and this proved not to be an easy task. Again, Chris Todd played a major role, since he was able to get great bands for Darwin's May Ball at a reasonable price. The price included strippers, which Chris kept as a surprise until the very moment of their performance, which is why I did not see them. That year, the Darwin May Ball was a success. It was sold out in advance and made a good profit.

*Francisco Guerra y Rullan*
DCSA Chairman 1973–4

Being part of the May Ball Committee in Darwin College in 2003–4 is the most treasured memory of my student days. We were lucky to have an extremely enthusiastic and committed group determined to put on the biggest party of the year. It was a wonderful feeling to know we could let our imagination run wild and then work out how we could share it with our College friends. We had a Hollywood theme and covered everything from Western movies on the island with tequila shots and a bucking bronco (we worried that someone might get thrown into the river), to the James Bond classics, with a casino in the Parlour.

Louisa Dunlop and Ben Lishman were in charge of the entertainment. They chose top local bands and DJs to play till dawn, and magician and hypnotist acts to captivate their audience long enough to have the largest survivors' photo ever taken in Darwin College.

The decoration team, Christina Soromani, Uma Mallya, Claire Skinner and Tom Cryer, transformed the atmosphere of the College into something enchanting, with fun references to Hollywood movies scattered across the grounds. They created new floors, covered ceilings and went mad with carpentry. My favourite touches were the white Hollywood sign on the bridge linking the two islands reflected in the river and the Batman symbol flashing every so often on the walls of the Dining Hall.

*Above: The 2004 May Ball Committee.*

*Danielle Bradshaw, Development Assistant,*
*designing decorations for the May Ball, 2012.*

*Queuing on Silver Street for the Darwin May Ball, 2012.*

Deborah Pino-Pasternak and Alex Head kept the troops fed and hydrated. We welcomed our guests with a glass of champagne. I still use the method taught me by our Bursar Peter Brindle for pouring efficiently the 900 glasses of champagne we had to serve in the first hour of the Ball. Apparently it is an important skill taught in the army! Tireless Mr Brindle himself served up breakfast after the Ceilidh at 6am.

Kam Nagpal and Derek Kam hired the 100 helpers without whom we couldn't have set up the grounds, tidied up and kept our guests safe. Amyas Phillips had a firm hand on all the accounts so that we could reimburse previous debts, give the best value for money to the guests and leave a little extra in case of problems in future May Balls.

Melanie Keene and Martyn Dade-Robertson, in charge of publicity and design respectively, made sure we were sold out of tickets weeks before the event so that we could splash out on extras such as providing a hot air balloon. It was a proud moment when Martyn showed a professional-level movie trailer at the launch bop in the College bar.

I want to thank again the College staff, who were so open-minded and trusting, letting us provide a decent party to celebrate the College members' hard work at the end of the academic year, and everyone on this committee for forgiving me for being so trigger happy with the walkie talkie on the night.

*Darwin May Ball 2012. The Bursar, Peter Brindle, acting as sommelier and bouncer.*

It is a Darwin tradition for the May Ball Committee to keep the theme secret until tickets are released at the launch party. We knew we could never keep it completely quiet, so to resolve this each committee member told one or two of their closest friends a different, fake theme, be it 'Lego dinosaurs' or 'Star Wars'. Within days everyone in College knew the theme. Or so they thought! We kept the real theme – *'cirque du soleil'* – quiet until the launch party and the ball was a success.

*Julia Zaccai*
May Ball President 2004

*Akin Ali*
May Ball President 2011

# THE FOUNDATION

## THE EARLY DAYS OF DARWIN COLLEGE
### John Bradfield

Like certain other notable events, the initial decision to attempt the creation of Darwin College happened in a railway carriage. It came about in this way: during the late 1950s and early 1960s a major campaign was mounted by Cambridge bursars and a few Oxford bursars to terminate the severely restrictive powers of the Ministry of Agriculture in relation to the management of college endowments under the Universities and College Estates Act 1925. This involved frequent journeys to London to negotiate with civil servants (and ultimately produced substantial emancipation under the similarly named Act of 1964).

The Cambridge leaders initially were John Boys Smith (Senior Bursar, St John's – an exceedingly wise academic theologian) and E.P. 'Sam' Weller (Senior Bursar, Gonville and Caius, doyen of the Cambridge bursars). By the early 1960s, however, Boys Smith had become Master of St John's, and the Cambridge group then consisted most frequently of Weller, Trevor Thomas (Senior Bursar, St John's), Ken (later Sir Kenneth) Berrill (First Bursar, King's College) and myself.

Simultaneously with the Estate Act negotiations there had been much debate in Cambridge over the need to make better provision for the award of college Fellowships to appropriate University Officers, who had been much increased in number with government finance after World War II. A University committee chaired by Lord Bridges was appointed to report on the relationship between the University and the colleges. One of its major recommendations was provision of more college Fellowships for University Officers in teaching and/or research. The committee's detailed scheme for achieving this was not accepted for several reasons, but numerous colleges responded positively by creating extra Fellowships. However, there was wide agreement that the aim could not be achieved solely by expansion of existing colleges. And fortunately the ancient college system was meanwhile showing remarkable vigour by generating spontaneously a dramatic outburst of new colleges. More were founded in the 20 years after World War II than in the 200 years before. Some (Churchill) were to commemorate an outstanding leader; some (Robinson) founded and others (Wolfson – originally founded by the University as University College) later named to commemorate outstanding benefactors; some (New Hall, now Murray Edwards after a generous benefactor, and Lucy Cavendish) to promote women's education; some (Clare Hall and Darwin) because it

*Opposite: Newnham Grange from the river.*

36

seemed the right thing to do in the light of the Bridges Report. Each had its special angle, but all made significant provision of extra Fellowships.

However, new foundations need a lot of founding – their creation requires a vast amount of time, thought and effort. In our own case it seemed to me that our small Estates group was an ideal body for proposing joint establishment of a new foundation by our four colleges. The group had forged great unity and loyalty in the fires of tough Estates Act negotiations. So I drafted a short note suggesting this idea and circulated it to my three bursar colleagues. We discussed it several times when we were conveniently gathered together on our way back from London by train following Estates Act meetings (discussions during the journey up were devoted to preparing for the meetings). It was on such a journey back from London in mid-1962 that the four of us decided to ask our colleges to adopt the idea. Final agreement to do so was reached while the train was halted by signals outside Cambridge station; our carriage, I well remember, was on that part of the line beside Rattee & Kett's yard, now part of Homerton. King's later decided not to join in (but has, of course, assisted the University in other ways). Caius, St John's and Trinity went ahead enthusiastically.

The earliest thoughts were for a college without students – a Cambridge All Souls as it were – in very specific response to that part of the Bridges Report which focused attention on the need for the provision of additional Fellowships. I do not know what transpired when the note was discussed at Caius and St John's, but I recall that when it came to the Trinity Council the first Lord Adrian (distinguished nerve-physiologist, Master and hence Chairman) made one of his rare major interventions in the discussion to suggest (in his modest, diffident and humorous manner) that the fellows of the new college ought to have students associated with them – for their mutual benefit. Probably others would in due course have suggested students if he had not, but so far as we are concerned he was the first to urge inclusion of a student body. He little knew that what was to become

Darwin would, as a result of the wisdom of him and others, gather the largest body of graduate members of any Oxbridge college.

I have vivid memories of the very happy – at times, indeed, hilarious – meetings in my room (H2 Great Court) between Sam Weller, Trevor Thomas and myself to draft the statutes and ordinances for the new college (following cordial agreement in principle between the three founding colleges). There was total harmony, each only too willing to see the others' point of view, moved as we were by enthusiasm for the project and friendship with one another.

Weller was a professional estate manager and had a tremendous reputation for knowledge and efficiency in bursarial matters – but had also a rather dour and tough exterior; yet under that exterior lurked a very humorous, friendly and harmonious character, which came to the fore here. Trevor Thomas was the soul of agreeable wisdom, tact and legal expertise. Both were great pillars of the Darwin cause in those early days. In due course Trevor Thomas was admirably succeeded by Christopher Johnson, who followed him as Senior Bursar of St John's, and possessed all the qualities required to carry on the good work. Let it also be recorded that we owed a major debt to John Horwood-Smart (of Taylor's, solicitors at

*Mark Pryor, Fellow of Trinity and son-in-law of Gwen Raverat.*

Newmarket, and now also Cambridge as Taylor Vinters), for the skilful and elegantly simple drafting of the Trust Deed, which was to govern operations until the Charter was granted.

At an early stage in our deliberations we were joined by the first Master of the College – Frank Young, Professor of Biochemistry. I proposed him to the Trustees not only because he had particularly advocated the creation of a graduate college (in a joint memorandum with Michael McCrum, then Master of Corpus and Vice-Chancellor), but also because I had much admired his chairmanship of the St Faith's School Committee which, by happy chance, I had been invited to join a few years earlier, soon after my son entered the school. As a Fellow of Trinity Hall, Frank had already proved his skill at combining scientific work and collegiate life. At Darwin he excelled in creating 'instant tradition'. He had just the qualities required by the young College, and he was soon joined by 12 good men and true – the first Fellows.

So the embryo developed, but it had no dwelling place or name. Here fortune took a hand again. The death of Sir Charles Darwin in 1962 had decided his family to vacate Newnham Grange and the Old Granary, and now Mark Pryor stepped into the picture. He was a highly original zoologist and Senior Tutor of Trinity. He loved a good joke, hated bureaucracy, and took an independent line about almost everything. Normally he approached you with a wicked twinkle in his eye describing, for example, how last Saturday afternoon he had taken out a party of his tutorial pupils collecting the more bizarre varieties of edible fungi and in the evening they had made a marvellous meal of their fried toadstools along with oysters and stout – and all survived (he was indeed a 'compleat biologist'). On this occasion, however, he spoke to me with an earnest and heart-warming helpfulness towards the young, homeless, nameless foundation. His wife, Sophie, was the daughter of Gwen Raverat (famous sometime denizen of the Old Granary), which

## THE POST-WAR HIGHER EDUCATION CONTEXT

Following the end of World War II several reviews of higher and further education had emerged from Whitehall; development in the sciences and appropriate provision for technology were seen to be of great importance. (In this latter Sir Charles [Galton] Darwin served on the committee which produced the *Percy Report 1945*.) Clearly expansion was going to be needed, but how should it be accommodated within the existing system of education? In 1956 a White Paper on technical education examined the relationship between technological colleges and universities: might they be integrated? Such discussions culminated in Lord Robbins' landmark report on higher education of 1963 in which government agreed that 'courses of higher education should be available to all those who are qualified by ability and attainment to pursue them and who wish to do so'. Expansion was now official policy.

Doubtless some insights into the thinking of Robbins' Committee had been gleaned around college tables during the report's two-year gestation. It was a propitious moment for Cambridge University and the future college. In 1960 a syndicate was set up under Lord Bridges to consider the relationship between the colleges and the University in the light of growing numbers of researchers for whom no college accommodation was possible. One outcome of these deliberations was the creation of a new graduate centre. The other was the proposal for a new college exclusively for graduates. St John's, Gonville and Caius, and Trinity in particular gave active support to this idea. Following the unexpected death of Sir Charles Darwin in 1962 the as yet unnamed graduate college acquired both a name and premises with the enthusiastic support of the Darwin family. It was the birth of Darwin College.

gave him close contacts with the Darwin family. During conversations in the Trinity Parlour after lunch, he suggested to me that the young College might seek to rent Newnham Grange and the Old Granary as a first home. We jumped at the idea.

Given Mark Pryor's splendid inspiration the next step was to head off the competition. The obvious (and eminently reasonable) rival was Queens'. The Bridges Report which had engendered our new College was also the *raison d'être* of the Colleges Committee, and it fortunately happened that Arthur Armitage (President of Queens') and I were members of the Colleges Committee's sub-committee on the Bridges Report. I well remember that after an evening meeting of the sub-committee at Peterhouse I asked Arthur Armitage if I could accompany him to Queens' and seek his views on an inter-college matter. He kindly agreed. In his study late that night I explained the urgent need of the young College for premises and the way in which it represented a vital response to the Bridges Report, which we had been discussing. Although a great go-getter for Queens' (and other worthy causes), Armitage kindly agreed not to press the claims of his college in respect of the Darwin home. So the way was clear. (Since then, of course, fortune has well rewarded the altruism of Queens' with benefactions

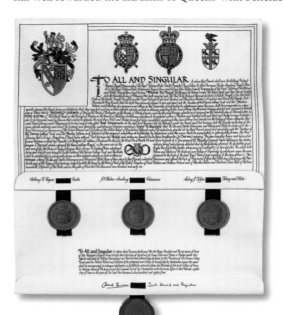

*The Darwin College Grant of Arms*

*Erasmus Darwin by Wright of Derby, one of several paintings belonging to the Darwin family which hang in the College.*

## THE DARWIN NAME

On New Year's Eve 1962, Sir Charles Galton Darwin, grandson of Charles Robert Darwin, died at Newnham Grange, the house which had been bought by his father, Sir George Howard Darwin. Lady Darwin and her family no longer wished to live in Cambridge and were approached by the consortium of colleges that were intending to establish a graduate college. When it was decided that the College should be named Darwin, the family agreed to allow the family coat of arms to be incorporated into the College's on the understanding that the College was to be named after the family and not solely Charles Robert. The same stipulation was made at Darwin College, University of Kent, to which my husband, George, who regularly graced their annual feast, donated a bust of Erasmus [Darwin]. A scholarship was set up in the name of Charles and Katharine Darwin and the family have lent several family portraits to the College, which include Erasmus Darwin by Wright of Derby, Charles Robert Darwin by W.W. Ouless and Charles Galton Darwin by his cousin, Robin Darwin.

*Angela Darwin*

*Founding Bursars – John Bradfield, John Boys Smith, Sam Weller and Trevor Thomas.*

of buildings and cash!) Accordingly, Lady Darwin and her family were approached, and they were immensely helpful. A lease was negotiated. Soon afterwards we had the happy idea of naming the infant foundation 'Darwin College'. Lady Darwin and her family were consulted again and they consented with enthusiasm. It was a great joy – and most appropriate – that she later became an Honorary Fellow of the College.

So Darwin College acquired a splendid home and a splendid name. Later Newnham Grange and the Old Granary were bought from the Darwin family, and St John's made the noble gesture of selling the Hermitage to the Darwin Trustees, thus extending the lovely riverside site in a most helpful manner. Subsequent action by energetic Darwin Bursars has much extended the College buildings.

There has been: construction of the Rayne Building, the Hall, the Library and an excellent hostel beside the mill-stream behind Newnham Mill; purchase across the road of the historic Malting House, with 14 rooms extending along the quaint Malting House Lane and a large rear garden; and the particularly significant purchase (singly or in groups) of the properties in Newnham Terrace, except the pub. (It should be noted that the pub would make a splendid student residence – and the combined gardens of the Newnham Terrace houses would make for a superb riverside site for a significant new residential building close to the heart of the College – all that's needed are generous benefactors, who could hardly have more attractive sites in which to be commemorated!)

Even fragmentary reminiscences, like these, about the early days of Darwin would be incomplete without reference to the key role of Michael Babington Smith (Trinity, matriculated 1920). He was senior London member of the Trinity Finance Committee in the 1960s (and for many years a Director of Glyn Mills, now part of the Royal Bank of Scotland, and of the Bank of England). When Darwin was up and running we naturally began to think of possibilities of further endowment. I called on Michael at Glyn Mills in Lombard Street, and described the background and the then state of play. He pondered the situation and then directed me to Sir Edwin Herbert (later Lord Tangley), a distinguished lawyer, public servant and highly respected City figure. I vividly recall visiting him in the gloomy, cavernous and labyrinthine old Winchester House, about 200 yards south of Liverpool Street Station, at the corner of Old Broad Street and Great Winchester Street. He was interested and sympathetic, but entirely non-committal. Only after a lapse of a few months did it transpire that he was a Trustee of the Rayne Foundation and that the Foundation was willing to consider helping Darwin. The tremendous assistance from the Foundation which followed is well known – and rightly commemorated in the name of the prominent Rayne Building. But it is splendid to have this further opportunity to record a warm acknowledgement of Darwin's profound gratitude to Max Rayne, his fellow Trustees and advisors, and his family – not only for their major financial help, but also for the immensely valuable encouragement and advice which they have given the College during its first half-century.

Darwin has succeeded far beyond the dreams of its founders. They cautiously envisaged a Master, no fewer than 40 Fellows and no fewer than 40 graduate members. The College now contains 65 Fellows and over 700 graduate members (and notably now has its first female Master, a former student of the College). Some 30 senior members of the University are associated with it in other ways. And it has made noble efforts to extend its facilities to a number of postdocs – an important class who can miss the huge educational benefits of interdisciplinary chat during College life, not being any longer students but also usually not being mature enough for Fellowships.

Meanwhile Darwin's main body, the graduate members, become ever more important in relation to the status of the University. Perish the thought that Cambridge should ever become a

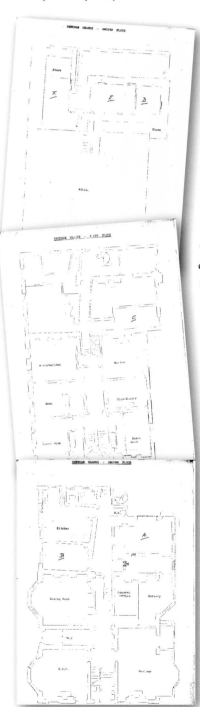

*Plans for the disposal of rooms, 1964.*

solely graduate university. It is vital for our national prosperity that we should have a steady stream of first-class undergraduates passing annually into our professions and commerce. But stratification of UK universities into 'research intensive' and 'teaching intensive' renders Darwin's large graduate body ever more important for maintenance of the University's high international reputation – as many of these graduates, recruited worldwide, play significant roles in University research teams. We need to keep a sharp eye on our competitor universities in this respect – especially as some rating agencies may take graduate student numbers as a proxy for research distinction. It is vital not to allow simple graduate numbers, or number and weight of publications, to overshadow quality.

Finally, it is important to record that Darwin has been exceedingly fortunate in having a steady flow of first-class College Officers – Masters, Vice-Masters, Bursars, Deans and others. It is they who have achieved such successful development on the base provided by the founders, benefactors and friends of Darwin. And it is they who have managed its resources with great skill and to such good effect. Long may the College continue to flourish, to receive great help from benefactors and other friends, and to benefit from serendipity in so many ways.

*The last meeting of the Nominative Trustees before the College achieved full independent status, 1976. L–R John Bradfield, Gordon Robin, Frank Young, John Boys Smith, Michael Crosthwait, Christopher Johnson and Air Commodore Frederick Moir Milligan.*

## SIR FRANK GEORGE YOUNG
### Elisabeth Leedham-Green

Some time before Darwin College was even a gleam in the eye of our founding fathers, Frank Young had been prominent in the University among those pressing for better provision for both tenured academics and post-doctoral workers without any college affiliation, and better provision also for graduate students. He was not the only person so concerned. In 1960 the University set up a syndicate under Lord Bridges, son of the poet Robert Bridges and a distinguished civil servant, ending his career as such as Head of the Home Civil Service. The syndicate's report in 1962 resulted soon after with the establishment of the Graduate Centre, built by the firm of Howell, Killick, Partridge and Amis (hereafter HKPA) which, a few years later, was to be responsible for our Hall and for the Rayne Building, as well as the refurbishment of the Hermitage. Matters, however, did not rest there. Frank, and another member of the syndicate, Dr John Smart, continued

to press for better collegiate provision. These early manoeuvres are described in some detail in Sir Frank's history of the College produced in 1967, and their result is covered in Sir John Bradfield's evocative account of the foundation of Darwin College above.

So, apart from his interest in provision for untenured staff and for graduate students, who was Frank Young? Most evidently he was Head of the Department of Biochemistry, and immensely distinguished as a scientist. A very good account of him in general can be found in Sir Philip Randle's obituary of him for the Royal Society (1990). Our concern here, however, is chiefly with his role as the first Master of the College. The College archives illustrate Sir Frank's hands-on style of management. Almost every document was filed not only in Darwin but at the Department of Biochemistry. Constant memoranda passed between him, the first Bursar, A.C. 'Bill' Stuart-Clark, the Nominative Trustees (representing the founding colleges) and the Rayne Trustees, at a rate of well over one a day.

These memoranda range from the vital (negotiations with architects, planning officials and the like) to what might now strike us as the trivial (better cigars, more ash-trays). Although nearly always benign in person, Sir Frank could be alarmingly severe on paper. Letters that most of us would only have written in our minds, were duly dictated, typed and sent. His portrait well represents this somewhat paradoxical nature. It has been said that he never looked

quite like that, but he did when shifting from one mode to the other. There is the smile and the twinkle alternating with the more austere model. Meetings of the Governing Body, which were often lengthy (a 10pm guillotine had to be introduced), were conducted with some ceremony, but while the proper protocols had to be observed, there was plenty of scope for discussion of general principles. The course of the good ship Darwin was open to negotiation, but the brass would be well polished and the decks well whited. For example, early plans of the disposition of rooms in Newnham Grange, the first part of the site to be occupied by the College, show a Senior Common Room, rooms for Fellows (the tiny number of graduate members being mostly accommodated in the Old Granary) and similar provisions with which Frank would have been familiar at Trinity Hall. All that had vanished by the early 1970s.

**Above:** *Frank Young by William Edward Narraway. The silver dish was presented to the College by Trinity Hall in honour of its first Master, Frank Young, and the silver stoops were presented by the Rayne Foundation.*

Frank's wife Ruth, meanwhile, a psychiatrist by profession, made it her concern to make female graduate members, and more particularly the wives of male ones, feel at home, and would hold lunch parties for them, for female Fellows and for Fellows' wives. In this she was aided and abetted, sometimes competitively, by Dr Sylvia Fitton Jackson, the first female Fellow, who mothered families in particular but also all those who were in need of help. Ruth organised lunches, Sylvia rallied round with gifts for newborn babies and help with accommodation. She could, and did, travel around the globe staying with one Old Darwinian family after another. From a Master and 12 Fellows in November 1964, by the time of Frank's retirement in September 1975, there were 40 Fellows, one Research Fellow and 272 graduate members in a college fully established and incorporated in the University and looking forward confidently to the future.

## THE FOUNDING FELLOWSHIP
### Abe Yoffe

Darwin College essentially was the brainchild of John Bradfield, then Bursar of Trinity College, and a group of colleagues, but the fact remains that without Frank Young's active and enthusiastic involvement Darwin would not have developed as it did.

As is clear from my letter of appointment in 1964, 12 of us, all male, were invited to become the founding Fellows of this new college to be called Darwin College. Frank Young, a biochemistry professor and Fellow of Trinity Hall, was to be the first Master. Although it was never stated, it seemed to me that the Trustees, particularly the Master of St John's, the Revd John Boys Smith, who was Chairman of the Trustees, saw the College as being an all-male establishment.

*Left: Early Fellows, c.1967. L–R Standing: Reg Goodwin, Ernest Childs, Gordon Robin, John Oates, Harold Whitehouse, Patrick Seuren, Alun Moelwyn-Hughes, Gerd Buchdahl. Seated: Graham Hough, John Smart, Frank Hayhoe, Frank Young, Philip McNair, 'Bill' Stuart-Clark, Jack Goodison.*

*Above:* Cambridge Evening News *report on the trial of the Hon. Mrs Jackson.*

*Above:* The College's first female Fellow, Sylvia Fitton Jackson, 1968.

Frank Young saw the College very much as his fiefdom and dispensed tasks to the Fellows in a manner he considered appropriate. It was Young's idea that Frank Hayhoe, a haematologist, should become the first Vice-Master, a position he held for many years. The general feeling was that Hayhoe was also being groomed to become Young's successor as Master, and this led to some unease later on.

We were given a building, Newnham Grange, the Old Granary and a vegetable garden, where our Study Centre now stands. We also acquired a housekeeper, the Hon. Mrs Jackson, a cordon bleu chef, although what was honourable about her was not at all clear to us as she finally finished up in jail, having fraudulently obtained credit at Eaden Lilley's and several other Cambridge shops. Our first Bursar, a retired, kindly and gentle ex-housemaster, one Stuart-Clark, was completely under the thumb of Mrs Jackson, and John Smart, one of our Scottish Fellows, was heard to remark that 'she fascinates him like a snake'. Young insisted we had regular meals together in Newnham Grange around the Talleyrand table, where we discussed how to proceed with the running of a college on very limited funds and limited grounds and facilities.

It was decided at the outset that we would be non-denominational with no chapel or high table, and that meals would be started by the senior Fellow

## MARIA REGINA TAVARES DA SILVA, 1966–7

Coming from Portugal in my university years I felt a great desire to see the world and enlarge my horizons. One schoolyear in the USA on a Fulbright scholarship was a first step in that direction. The experience of two years in Cambridge proved to be the next, and my belonging to Darwin became a significant part of that experience.

As I came to Cambridge in 1965, Darwin College was not part of my plans. I came as a Lectrice in Portuguese to the Faculty of Modern Languages, Sidgwick Avenue, and stayed there for two years; it was only in the second year that belonging to Darwin became part of my life.

I enrolled for a Diploma in English Studies, under the guidance of Professor Graham Hough, and was quite pleased by the opportunity to become a member of Darwin. It was a new, special college, graduate-only, and open for men and women, in a very particular setting, and with a family atmosphere. I did not live there, but came often for dinner and for socialising, for exchanging ideas and views, for meeting new people and making new friends.

In the States during the schoolyear of 1963–4, I had experienced an exciting time, with the enthusiasm for the civil rights movement and the quest for equal rights for all. I was there at the time of the Great March on Washington, and the ideals of democracy and equality – namely equality of women and men – became central to my way of thinking and envisaging a new social order.

In Cambridge in general and in Darwin specifically, these notions gained new roots; I recall the informal discussions – mostly at the dinner table – and the really diverse views on many central issues of a social and political nature.

Also in Cambridge, and in my Darwin year, I met my future husband, who was doing his PhD in chemical Engineering, and fortunately we are still together. We went to the College, enjoyed the rituals of academic life at the time, ventured into punting on the river, took pictures in the wonderful settings of the gardens … so many memories!

Soon after returning home, I ended my short teaching career and changed the course of my professional life. For many years now I have been active in a field for which my years abroad, both in the States and in Cambridge, helped to pave the way. It is the field of equality of women and men, envisaged as a prerequisite for the achievement of genuine democracy and as a requirement of human rights.

I chaired the national mechanism for equality in the government of my country, entrusted with the political responsibility in this field; I also chaired the intergovernmental Committee for Equality of the Council of Europe and the Advisory Committee of the European Commission on the same issue. At UN level, for eight years, I was an elected member of the Treaty Body dealing with these matters – the Convention on the Elimination of All Forms of Discrimination Against Women, better known as the CEDAW Convention.

If my American experience started to open a window, the Cambridge days and my Darwinian year helped to keep it open and alert. Something to be grateful for!

---

present in the simplest manner, ignoring ideas from Moelwyn-Hughes that we stood for a minute's silence, like the Quakers, and finishing up with the current *Benedictus Benedicat*.

When it came to electing new Fellows, Young favoured those with medical, biological or biochemical backgrounds, and Derek Bendall was one of our new recruits. In this way we probably lost out on a number of distinguished candidates in other subjects who would have accepted Fellowships, but with all the delays brought about by the setting up of sub-committees and all the long-winded discussions, potential Fellows could be

## MEMORIES OF DARWIN AND THE OLD GRANARY, 1965–6

My best memories of Darwin College are of my mates in English in the Old Granary and some of the elders across the garden in the main house. Chris Bristow, Pat Parrinder and I were supposed to be reading English. Pat actually managed to get a lot done. Chris, no doubt, attended classes and lectures, too, but what I remember best is his clandestine adventure with the mysterious Sandra of Sardinia, who we all liked and referred to as the 'Dottoressa'. I don't know if Sandra already had her degree, but that is what we called her.

Philip McNair, who was then Dean, and so charged with our moral welfare, was, as I recall, quite upset about Chris's sometime live-in arrangement. Chris and Pat were rather down on Philip for interfering with our pleasures, but I remained very fond of him. I was touched by his solicitude for me, which extended to introducing me to a nice Jewish girl from Leeds and Girton so that I wouldn't feel lonely. It didn't click, but I was grateful for Philip's concern.

My supervisor was Graham Hough. Graham was perfect in a wholly different way. He must have been aware that I wasn't working very hard, but he seemed to take the view that Americans on a one-year visit ought to be able to work or chase women or see the countryside or whatever else they pleased. Sometime during my year at Darwin Graham wrote a piece for *The Listener* on Lionel Trilling's new book *Beyond Culture*. He was very tough on the book. As an admirer of Trilling, I was offended by Graham's review, although in later years I have come to agree with most of what he said. In any case, my upset with Graham's essay was one element in my decision some ten years later to write a book of my own on Trilling. I'm glad to say that Graham liked my book, because he knew Trilling's work very well and, apart from that review, was one of Trilling's great champions in England.

Pat Parrinder was already quite formidable in 1965–6. He greeted me on our first meeting – or so I remember it – with a fierce denunciation of American actions in Vietnam. Since I was so benighted as to know next to nothing about what these actions were, I was rather nonplussed by Pat's fierceness. Despite the fact of my original-sinfulness as a Yank, we did become friends and have seen each other frequently in the years since.

There were others, too, like Philip Grover, who was then writing his dissertation on James under Graham's supervision, but Philip was married and lived out, so I don't identify him so closely with the College. But I hope someone else will talk about our Spanish maid and our dignified Polish butler and the snapped up by other colleges when they got wind of the fact that they were possible candidates for Darwin.

The introduction of women into the College took place by the drip-feed process. A female medical graduate member was first admitted, and the Trustees said nothing. We then went a little further and elected Sylvia Fitton Jackson from the Strangeways Laboratories as a Fellow, and again the Trustees made no comment, and the procedure escalated from then on.

There were some real characters among the founding Fellows, and I would single out a few, namely Graham Hough, a lecturer in English, who was an entertaining character with a waspish tongue, and an extreme left-winger who saw a 'CIA man' in every new American graduate member or visitor to the College. He could not bear long-winded statements at meetings, very much the style of Frank Young, where he would eventually bang the table, with 'I can't stand this any longer', and walk out. Another was John Oates, the Under-Librarian at the University Library, a Latin scholar with a distinctive voice and a fund of good common sense, and John Smart, a large Scot who was an expert on insects and who gave us the gong in the Hall.

very grave and gentle medical student – I can't recall his name – who occasionally showed up for dinner. Dons and students ate together in that first year. Meals were cheap, but conversation did not always get off the ground. One exception was the visit of Isaiah Berlin, who was then planning Wolfson College at Oxford, and came over to learn from our example. Graham also was a great talker, but my memory is of his only very rarely dining in Hall.

– *Mark Krupnick, Darwin College Magazine No.4, 1989*

*Mark Krupnick (1939–2003) was a Fulbright scholar at Darwin in 1965–6 and became Professor of Religion and Literature at the University of Chicago, where in 2000 he was struck down by amyotrophic lateral sclerosis (Lou Gehrig's disease). He died two years later at the age of 63.*

*Mark, Chris Bristow, and I were among the seven new research students who moved into the Old Granary in the autumn of 1965; the others included the distinguished physicist John Clarke, the Arctic explorer Julian Paren and Bill Shea, then a Catholic priest. What had brought me to Darwin was a report in the student newspaper* Varsity *some months earlier that the College wanted to include some Cambridge graduates among its first student intake. Philip McNair had not yet taken over as Dean so I found*

*myself being interviewed by Graham Hough, who had been one of my second-year supervisors at Christ's. We got on very well – much better than we had ever done at Christ's – and, as he escorted me downstairs after the interview, Graham slapped me on the back and confided, 'I was getting so bored with teaching undergraduates'. I already knew that, of course, but it was the best possible welcome to Darwin. Yes, it was still Cambridge – but a very different Cambridge.*

*The Vietnam War was not yet at its height, but the University in 1965 was full of American graduate members, one reason being that they wanted to keep a distance from their draft boards. This is the background to the political argument that Mark so vividly remembered. Among the 'elders' he recalled, I would think of Frank Young, John Oates, Jack Goodison and several others who went out of their way to be kind to us. The 'grave and gentle medical student' was, of course, Chester White. My first meeting with Chester came in the Long Vacation of 1965, when he was busily sandpapering the second-hand desks that were to be installed in our rooms in the Old Granary; for a moment I took him to be the College carpenter. Later he restored a dilapidated old punt and showed us how to handle it, a skill which once learnt is never forgotten.*

**Patrick Parrinder**

Finally, I have to say that the College has developed beyond my wildest dreams. Apart from the Rayne Foundation bequest, one important event stands out for me. This was the appointment of Moses Finley as our second Master. An ancient historian, he brought scholarship and intellectual rigour to the College, and it flourished during his tenure.

*The gong in the Dining Hall, given by John Smart, one of the first Fellows.*

## DEREK POCOCK, 1969–70

While working as a Forensic Pathologist at St
George's Hospital, I began to feel that some serious
knowledge of crime in its widest sense would be an
asset when giving evidence on the various criminal
matters which were my daily workload. So I was
granted a sabbatical year from the medical school
conditional upon my working during the vacations at
my regular duties in London.

I was accepted by the Institute of Criminology
and applied to Darwin as a postgraduate student for
residence. Here I was able to have the double room, as
the building was then divided, in the Old Granary – that
was the area with the rickety balcony.

Life in Darwin was quite idyllic. We had a kitchen
and my co-habitees were a MoD explosives expert who
was often off on secret assignments, a volcanologist and
an English expert on some abstruse author.

I was also fortunate to have a car since I had
regular trips to London to give evidence on cases I had
done in the past year. This was also valuable for our
frequent trips from the Institute of Criminology to
prisons, as I could assist with giving lifts to my fellow
students.

*Graham Hough, who
was officially but
briefly the College's
first Dean.*

*Bill Stuart-Clark,
first Bursar.*

## COMPUTER SCIENCE

*David Wheeler, Fellow 1965–94.*

Darwin has been home to several important figures in the world of computing. David Wheeler was a pioneer in computing. As an undergraduate reading mathematics at Trinity College he heard about the EDSAC computer being built by Maurice Wilkes and his team and went along to help with the construction. He showed great interest in the programming proposals and made valuable contributions. He was involved in the selection of the mnemonic code for the instructions and noticed errors in the provisional start-up orders.

With a DSIR grant and a Trinity award he became a research student and developed the programming system which came into use in May 1949. He wrote the initial orders which allowed a program written in simple code

with decimal addresses to be read into the machine. He was also responsible for the development of the library of mathematical functions and print routines and invented a clever way of calling them from the main program. He wrote the first programs including a table of squares (results printed in decimal) and his first useful program was to search for prime numbers. The EDSAC was the first modern stored-program computer to provide a computing service and was widely used for University projects. His PhD was the first in the Computer Laboratory and led to a Trinity Fellowship.

Before taking up his Fellowship he spent two years at the University of Illinois at Champaign-Urbana and helped with the commissioning of the ILLIAC. He had successive University appointments, ending as the first Professor of Computer Science, and had the distinction of being elected to the Royal Society.

With the experience of EDSAC a new project for a successor, EDSAC2, was underway when he returned to the laboratory and David was entrusted with the design of the programming instructions, the control unit and fixed store which were held in magnetic core storage. It was now possible to include the basic functions in the fixed store and to allow the programs to be printed out by teleprinter, which made the new machine much easier to use. Again, David was very helpful to other users and wrote a Fast Fourier Transform program for the radio astronomers which led to a Nobel Prize for Martin Ryle. EDSAC2 was his favourite machine as he had no problems with compatibility, and his experience in both hardware and software meant that he could design for the needs of University researchers.

Soon it became clear that more computing power was needed, and cooperation with Ferranti for the purchase of some of the Atlas components led to the Titan computer. David was the design authority and early on it became clear that an online system was possible which led to major changes in the hardware. He designed a multiplexor to connect terminals to the computer. Although he wrote disc transfer programs the main software was written by others in the laboratory. Titan came into general use in 1967.

In 1966 he spent a well-earned sabbatical leave at the University of California, Berkeley. It was a happy family time, allowing many weekend trips around the state. He designed a multiplexor for the Berkeley system which enabled hundreds of teletypes to be connected to their CDC 6500 computer. It was in use for many years.

He had been without a college Fellowship for some years while very busy with computer development, so he was very pleased to be elected to a Fellowship at Darwin in 1965. It was very suitable as well, as he was always interested in research students and the quality of Cambridge students was a great pleasure to him.

He was involved in all the further developments in the Computer Laboratory including the Cambridge Ring, for which he designed and commissioned the first version. In his later years he returned to programming and set up a security group. Looking at data compression he invented an algorithm known as BWT (Burrows–Wheeler Transform – developed with his student Mike Burrows). It is now a standard technique for transferring data securely.

His retirement years were blighted by failing eyesight which made social contacts difficult. He continued to be happiest in the Computer Lab writing programs and contributing to seminars. An annual Wheeler lecture has been established in his memory.

*Joyce Wheeler*

Karen Spärck Jones was elected a Fellow in 1968 and became College Librarian in 1974. She remained at Darwin for 12 years before resigning her Fellowship and moving to Wolfson College. She began her research in the Cambridge Language Research Unit in the 1950s with Margaret Masterman and Roger Needham, who later became her husband. This work looked at thesauri in language information processing, specifically devising more accurate ways of distinguishing between ambiguous synonyms by classification into type clusters. Her research in information retrieval was to have major applications with the invention of the World Wide Web and became fundamental in techniques applied in Web search engines. After her migration to Wolfson, her research looked at relevance weighting for terms. Her later work focused on document and multimedia information retrieval as well as speech applications and information and language system evaluation. She became Professor of Computers and Information in 2000 and was the winner of many awards, most notably perhaps the Lovelace Award of the British Computer Society in 2007, the previous recipient of which was Tim Berners-Lee. She remains the only woman to have been given this award and she was a strong advocate for women in computing. An annual Karen Spärck Jones Lecture is held by the BCS, the Chartered Institute for

*Karen Spärck Jones, Fellow 1968–80.*

*Judy Bailey, Fellow
1968–84.*

IT, to honour women in computing research. She was a Fellow of the British Academy, of which she was Vice-President from 2000 to 2002.

Although not a computer researcher, Judy Bailey was known to thousands of computer users and others in the University, and was instrumental with her colleagues in providing Cambridge with some of the best computing facilities in the academic world. She came to Cambridge to take the Diploma in Numerical Analysis and Automatic Computing, which she was awarded in 1961. After one year of research, she found she was more cut out to become a programmer supporting research, so she joined a Cambridge research group employing computational techniques to support research. In her case it was Radio Astronomy, in those days under the pioneer Professor Sir Martin Ryle. She then joined the Mathematical Laboratory to assist Eric Mutch, the Superintendent of Computing Services, in the administration of computing facilities then provided by the laboratory to the whole University. In 1968 she was elected to a Fellowship in Darwin. Not long after, Eric Mutch suddenly died, and she found herself promoted into his post, reporting directly to the Director of the Laboratory, Sir Maurice Wilkes.

The Mathematical Laboratory was re-organised in 1970, and the University Computing Service was established as a formal entity with its own director. Thus began a singular career for her in the administration of University computing. She became Deputy Director and remained in that position until she retired in 1988. Her task of sharing the resources of a single computer among so many users in a fair and effective way required some clever administrative mechanisms which were developed by computing service programmers. Nevertheless, someone (or some persons) had to allocate the resources, and this fell to Judy, a task that she undertook more or less on her own. For all the advanced technology employed by the Computing Service in those years, Judy was the one person to interface that technology with almost half the Cambridge University population of academics, staff and students. At the same time, she would deal briskly with the early manifestations of the hacker culture, and with those she thought were pushing their luck too far.

*CW and Dr David Hartley*

# The Masters

## PASSING ON THE BATON

### Derek Bendall

I was one of the first group of three elected Fellows, who joined the existing twelve founding Fellows at the College in April 1965. Of these three, Philip McNair was an Italian scholar who became Dean soon after his election, I am a biochemist, and the third was Ieuan Harris, a protein chemist. Early on Harris was in the Biochemistry Department with Fred Sanger and had moved with him to the newly established MRC Laboratory of Molecular Biology; he later died in a tragic accident.

The foundation of Darwin College was an educational experiment, which took time to mature into the distinct and successful form we have today. In 50 years the College has grown far beyond the initial concept of 40 Fellows and 40 graduate members. The College has stuck firmly to the rule that it would accept only graduate students. In the early days this meant that almost all the student members were carrying out research. Each student's work was overseen by a supervisor appointed by the University Board of Graduate Studies, an arrangement that left no role for the College. (By contrast, the core activity of the traditional college was the supervision of undergraduates' work by fellows of the college.) Of course, the furtherance of research in a wide variety of topics, and the stimulus offered by Fellows and graduate members alike meeting together to discuss ideas, over a meal

perhaps, was of immense importance. Nevertheless, these benefits were intangible and not invariably realised, a situation which left a small number of Fellows sufficiently uneasy to resign. Inevitably there were also one or two who hankered after the more familiar social life offered by the high table and senior combination room of a traditional college.

It was Moses Finley, succeeding Frank Young in the Mastership when the College was still not quite a teenager, who gave the College a sense of intellectual dynamism and academic self-confidence. This grew out of several of Moses' initiatives, chief of which were the election of the first Research Fellows and the institution of the annual Darwin lecture by an outstanding guest speaker. His Mastership was crowned by the week-long Darwin Centenary Conference held in early summer 1982.

Moses Finley left a firm basis on which his successor, Arnold Burgen, could build. At first Arnold tried to replicate the success of the Darwin Conference, until Andy Fabian suggested the winning formula of a series of eight Friday afternoon lectures in the Lent Term on a topic of general interest which could be tackled by a series of outstanding speakers from all points of the academic compass. As a result of Andy Fabian's skilful leadership the annual Darwin

**Opposite:** *Portrait of Moses Finley, Master 1976–82, by Michael Noakes.*

College Lecture Series (eventually replacing the one annual lecture instituted by Moses Finley) has become a Cambridge institution capable of filling not only the largest lecture theatre in the city but one or even two overspill halls as well.

Finally, I may say that in my experience the graduate members are almost invariably happy in Darwin, valuing the informal, homely atmosphere. For this we must thank the wisdom of the founding Fellows and the first Master. Darwin cannot always match the provision for the practical needs of students available in the older, wealthier and more spacious colleges. But this is compensated by the beauty of Darwin's riverside site and garden.

*Right: The Chancellor visited Darwin in February 1986 and was entertained by the Master, Sir Arnold Burgen. Having held the Chair of Sheild Professor of Pharmacology for nine years, Arnold Burgen left teaching to serve as Director of the National Institute for Medical Research in 1971. In 1982, he was elected Master of Darwin and oversaw the instigation in 1986 of the Darwin College Lecture Series before retiring in 1989. He was elected a Fellow of the Royal Society in 1964 and served as its Foreign Secretary before helping to found the Academia Europaea in 1988.*

*Above: Moses Finley with Albert Einstein and Rabbi Stephen Samuel Wise (left), leader of the American Zionist Movement, the American Jewish Congress and the Jewish World Congress, late 1930s. Moses Finley was very active in the struggle to alert the American public to the dangers of Nazism. This activism led him to be suspected of Communist sympathies and to fall foul of the House Committee on Un-American Activities after the war, which ended his academic career in the USA when he was fired from his post at Rutgers University. He wrote to Albert Einstein in 1953 in an attempt to enlist his help but Einstein was unable to intervene and Moses Finley subsequently left the USA.*

## MOSES AND MARY FINLEY

*Born Moses Finkelstein in 1912, Moses Finley was a child prodigy. He graduated from High School in New York in two years and was the youngest freshman in any American college when he entered Syracuse University at the age of 11. He arrived in Cambridge as a University Lecturer in Classics in 1955 and revitalised the study of ancient social and economic history. He took British citizenship in 1962 and was elected a Fellow of the British Academy in 1971. He was Professor of Ancient History from 1970 to 1979 and Master of Darwin from 1976 to 1982.*

*Below is an extract from a tribute paid by the then Vice-Master, Professor D.H. Mellor, during the Finley Memorial Concert in the Music School, West Road, on Sunday 26 October 1986.*

When Moses became Master we were well established, and almost full grown, but still unsure of our role – a role of course less easily defined than that of a college which exists to teach undergraduates. By the time Moses retired our role was defined, not in words but in practice. It was defined, for example, in the expansion of our Research and Visiting Fellowships and Associateships, in our Colloquia and the activities of our College groups, and in our Annual Darwin Lectures. All of our activities were defined by the standards that Moses set us, and made us set ourselves, standards that would tax far larger and better endowed institutions. I, for instance, still recall my mounting alarm at the sheer scale of the Darwin Centenary Conference in 1982 in this very Hall, a conference that Moses casually talked me into spending two years organising. But now, as in our newer Darwin College Lecture Series, our Fellows take this kind and scale of College activity for granted.

We do so largely because of the expectations Moses and Mary excited in us, and the way in which they did so. Their last great gift to us, leaving us Moses' library, and his estate, to endow a Research Fellowship in Ancient History, is a typical combination of generosity and challenge. It is very like my colleague Elisabeth Leedham-Green's description of meeting Moses in a College corridor: the welcoming smile – and the sudden need to have one's wits about one. Our best memorial to Moses and Mary Finley would be to remain a place of which that is an apt description.

**Footnote:**

*It was Moses, ably abetted by Reg Goodwin and Sandy Robertson and by representatives of other colleges, who directed the attention of the University at large to the plight of PhD students who were overrunning, when 'in some Faculties [a student's] chance of completing in three years are virtually zero, and of completing in seven years 50 per cent and sometimes less'. At the time it appeared that the contribution to the discussion of Sir Geoffrey Elton, who laid all the blame on child-bearing, had scuppered any chance of amendment in the situation, but within a few years the point had been taken, and completion times were reduced.*

ELG

## 1989–2000: A PERSONAL VIEW
### Geoffrey Lloyd

When I came to Darwin in 1989 I had already been a Fellow of King's for over 30 years. The contrast with that college is perhaps the easiest way for me to pinpoint what I found distinctive about Darwin. King's was rich, fractious and very self-centred. Darwin was poor (our endowment at the time was less than the annual investment income of King's), friendly and unpretentious. At King's I had been used to College Council and Governing Body meetings that could go on for three to four hours. At Darwin the Council – a much smaller body with a higher proportion of graduate members – met at 6pm, and Hall was at 7.15. That concentrated the mind. The Darwin Governing Body meets after supper and takes about the same amount of time.

What money we had we spent, I believe, to excellent effect. The Darwin College Lecture Series did not at that time benefit from the munificence of Richard King, but for a modest outlay it made a considerable contribution to the intellectual life of the University and the city. By

When I came to Darwin the College had been in existence for a little over a decade and had obtained its independence under Royal Charter the year I arrived. Election to Darwin was a big and somewhat daunting leap from the rather uncertain life of a graduate in an undergraduate college, writing up and eking out a living as Newnham Primary School's lollipop man (a job I loved), to being a Fellow, if only a very junior and temporary one. What I remember most was how welcoming my new colleagues were. I was made to feel that I had a place at Darwin and that I was indeed a member of the community. Graciousness started at the top with the Master, the gravel-voiced, chain-smoking Moses Finley, who always seemed to have time for a word and whose intellectual eminence was obvious but somehow unremarkable and unremarked, at least by him; and with Brigadier Crosthwait, the Bursar, and Sylvia Fitton Jackson, alarming but very kind. I remember others with great fondness: George Gömöri, Chester White, Mario di Gregorio, with whom I started the History Group, the forerunner of the lunchtime seminars, Dean Hawkes and Hugh Mellor, Paul Kratochvil, Paul Ries and Sandy Robertson, the latter a fellow Africanist, Dick Holmes and John Oates, who both combined a magisterial command of University business with a sharp humour. It may have been because Darwin itself was still in the process of becoming a college community and because most people were department-based or had come from 'somewhere else', but it was their collective example that made me realise that a Fellowship was a society, a collection of individuals in all their variety of opinions, habits and enthusiasms. It was something to savour over sherry or by the river. In 1979 I left Darwin for Clare Hall and then left Cambridge for good, but it was at Darwin that, in the nicest way, I ceased to be a graduate and started to become an academic – which I still am.

*Geoffrey Lloyd,*
*Master 1989–2000,*
*with Mary Fowler,*
*Master since 2012.*

the late 1980s the success of the early series made it easy to attract stellar speakers. Introducing them was relatively easy, a matter of doing one's homework. Summing up at the end, in the days before each lecturer was supposed to provide an abstract in advance, could be scary. But it wasn't often that I had to invent what I thought the speaker should have said or meant. They were exciting occasions, and they gave us a marvellous opportunity to learn about a wide range of subjects well beyond what the University curricula generally cover.

We learnt too about the human qualities of many of our famous speakers. Archbishop Tutu and Shirley Williams were among those who, on entering the Hall for the formal dinner after the lecture, insisted on first saying hello to the Butler (Omar) and those of the kitchen staff who were there to greet them. It was heartening to see the great and the good appreciate those who work behind the scenes, not just ensuring that the College runs smoothly, but also making a major contribution to that friendly

atmosphere I referred to. I confess I must have aggravated my super-efficient Master's secretary, Joyce Graham, on many occasions – but she was always the soul of discretion.

Our most urgent need, in 1989, was to improve our library and IT facilities, up till then cramped in the two small rooms that now form the Old Library. There was controversy in the city and some in the College about the wisdom of using the narrow strip of land next to the Old Granary for a new Study Centre. But it had been derelict for some time and research showed that it had once been used for coal bunkers and warehousing for the horse-drawn barges that came up the Cam to the Mill Pond. The Dixon-Jones design we commissioned was, I thought, a stunner. Although initially the City's Planning Committee turned it down, we gritted our teeth and won on appeal – to the immeasurable benefit of generations of graduate members.

That building, and the others that followed in my time (Frank Young House, Gwen Raverat House, the purchase of No.1 and then of 9–12 Newnham Terrace), would have been impossible but for the massive support we received from the Rayne Foundation and from Trinity (where John Bradfield continued to be a staunch ally). I remember vividly when I first took Lord Rayne (who knew a thing or two about property development) into the Study Centre. His face lit up in positive amazement and delight, a reaction that almost every visitor shares. We had asked him whether he would like the building named after him: certainly not, he replied. The College has indeed been fortunate in its benefactors.

Buildings are important, people even more so. We worked hard at increasing the Research Fellowships we could offer, both stipendiary and non-stipendiary. By good bursarial management, we were able to double the numbers of those appointed to Mary and Moses Finley Fellowships and to Adrian Fellowships and new support from Schlumberger enabled us to add another stipendiary Fellowship. The Research Fellows as a whole are very good at throwing themselves into College life, and as organisers and inspirers they continue to be fundamental to the success of the lunchtime seminars as well as to the Lecture Series.

Our small official Fellowship played their cards in different ways. Roger Whitehead, who took over from Reg Goodwin as Vice-Master, and who proved incredibly loyal and helpful, used to distinguish between lunchtime Fellows and dinnertime ones. The main difference from King's, to use that contrast yet again, was that official Fellows did not gripe when asked to serve on this or that committee, to take on this or that office. I suppose we did not often ask those who were of a less collegial temperament, but we very rarely faced a 'no'. We tried hard to build up a Fellowship that had representatives from every discipline, though not always with complete success.

I have yet to mention the most important component of our community: our graduate members

*The Study Centre, which was built early in Geoffrey Lloyd's Mastership after a battle with the local planning authorities.*

FROM THE MASTER
PROFESSOR SIR GEOFFREY LLOYD FBA

DARWIN COLLEGE
CAMBRIDGE CB3 9EU
TEL: 01223-335666
FAX: 01223-335667
E-mail: gel20@hermes.cam.ac.uk

*14 July 2000*

*Dear Mihirinie Dear Kevin Dear Alice*

*Ji and I were both touched and overwhelmed by your lovely presents — the Orthoceras will have pride of place in our salon at 2 Prospect Row and the origin of stories will always be a reminder (as if we shall need it!!) of our time at Darwin. We have enjoyed the 11 years tremendously — thanks very largely to the great atmosphere that you and your predecessors have created in the college. It's a very special environment and has meant and will continue to mean a very great deal for everyone who has had the good fortune to be associated with it — me included! So a great thank you from both of us to you, your colleagues, your predecessors — and with very best wishes for your own future careers...*

*As ever Geoffrey + Ji*

*Letter to Mihirinie Wijayawardene, DCSA President, after the DCSA invited Sir Geoffrey and his wife to a farewell tea party.*

drawn from scores of different countries, bringing widely varying experience and interests to their work in Cambridge. An anecdote will serve to bring out the more than just academic impact of our collegiality. At the height of the war in the former Yugoslavia, we happened to have three female graduate members, one from Serbia, one from Bosnia, one from Croatia. They became good friends. Every day they heard appalling reports of danger and destruction to their homes and families. It was truly moving to see how their friendship remained unshaken, and indeed became stronger throughout those long traumatic days.

Actually, the very first group of people I got to meet on the first day of my Mastership was the DCSA committee under the chairmanship of J.D. Hill, who had invited me and my wife Ji to brunch in the Old Granary.

## JOYCE GRAHAM

'Continuity' has become my middle name at Darwin! And having worked with four of our six Masters I think I have probably earned it. I came to Darwin in January 1977, following a year in the USA. My return to Cambridge presented me with an opportunity to do something 'interesting' with my time, and interesting my time at Darwin certainly proved to be for the next 30 years.

Sir Moses Finley had just taken over as Master, having announced on appointment, 'No, I don't need a secretary – just give me a typewriter.' I began working with him three months later. Moses instituted the Annual Darwin Lectures and introduced some fascinating people to the College at a time when student numbers were rapidly increasing and becoming ever more international.

One particularly poignant memory that springs to mind at that time is of going into the Television Room and finding Arab and Israeli students with their arms around each other, weeping together at the scenes of violence on the newsreel footage of the war.

When Sir Arnold Burgen arrived he was Foreign Secretary of the Royal Society and during that time we had a succession of British Ambassadors and Consuls visiting for scientific briefings prior to taking up their foreign postings. Arnold, together with Andy Fabian, instituted the Darwin College Lecture Series, bringing into the College specialists in so many fields and attracting both local sixth-form college students, who did projects around our series, and senior members of the University.

Working with Sir Geoffrey Lloyd was a different challenge. Geoffrey was always in the midst of the largest group of graduate members in the Dining Hall every lunchtime. Extricating him on occasion was more than a little difficult. Tales of his olive-growing activities in Spain were quite legendary, and the olive oil sampling on his return always a pleasure.

I retired from Darwin during Professor Willy Brown's time having spent seven very happy years working with him, meeting Trade Union colleagues when he was an ACAS Conciliator and spending many a coffee break chatting about his beloved Yorkshire and my Northumberland.

The College played an important part in our family life too. My husband and I were lucky enough to be invited to so many of the College social occasions, and my husband gave a lecture in the lunchtime seminar series one year. The armillary sundial which stands in the College grounds is dedicated to his memory. My three boys were well known to members too. One of them rowed in the bumps one year when the crew was a member short – they won their blades that year! Another of my sons when he was very young had the honour of being taught how to play chess by Moses; in later years he spent his university vacations working with our Clerk of Works.

From the very first day I walked into Darwin, I have always felt privileged to work in its happy and stimulating environment, in the company of such eminent Fellows and Masters. So when I came to retire in January 2007 it was obvious that my gift to myself had to be a trip to the Galapagos.

*The armillary sundial presented to the College by Joyce Graham in memory of her husband, Gil.*

*Joyce Graham, Master's Secretary 1977–2007.*

They also invited Bob Sloss, the Dean. They may have thought they would need someone to break the ice. But that wasn't really necessary – as I think they soon realised. The DCSA has a crucial role in running all sorts of activities in the College, of course, and I recall with pleasure working with successive Chairs and officers. When my wife and I woke up in 2000 to find it was time to move on (and I am a great believer that one should retire, even though I felt anything but ready to leave), a group of past and present Chairs, Mihirinie, Kevin and Alice, organised a farewell party for us. Our happy experience at Darwin owes a great deal to them, as well as to the Fellowship and to the unfailingly efficient staff. The College has a very distinctive character, like no other institution I can think of. No one planned exactly what we should stand for – that has emerged from successive initiatives by individuals and groups. But as an example of what a college can be we have something quite special to offer, and long may we continue to do so.

## BEING MASTER
### Willy Brown

It is the educational aspect of Darwin College that I particularly treasure. It is not the graduate members' education that I refer to, but my own. For someone with omnivorous curiosity it was wonderful. As Master for a dozen years I have eaten my lunch at over 400 research talks by graduate members and Fellows. I have listened to nearly a hundred Lecture Series performances with the anxious attention that comes of having to say 'thank you' at the end. And there have been the myriad conversations about other people's research that come as part of everyday dining, degree congregations, formal halls and so on. It may have the superficiality of intellectual tourism, but was no less fascinating for that.

The Mastership was also the route to a unique involvement with Cambridge University. Working with the 30 other Heads of House is itself remarkable and, in a literal sense, collegial. It would be hard to find so diverse a range of talent and achievement elsewhere on the planet; but that does not mean that they find the arcane complexity of the University easy. I took to heart the advice that the best way to understand it is to get involved in it, and could have won records for committee membership. But I am sure that is one reason why I found so worthwhile my final incarnation, being Head of the School of Humanities and Social Sciences. In combination with my Darwin role, it provided an extraordinary insight into the wonders and workings of an extraordinary university.

*Professor Willy Brown, Master 2000–12. Before coming to Cambridge, Willy Brown was Director of the ESRC's Industrial Research Unit at Warwick. In 1980 he became Montague Burton Professor of Industrial Relations at Cambridge and a fellow of Wolfson College. He was on the ACAS Council for many years and served as an official ACAS arbitrator for more than 20 years.*

## JENNY EDMONDS, 1968–81

I arrived in Cambridge in the autumn of 1968 to take up an SRC postdoctoral Fellowship in the Botany School after completing my PhD at the University of Birmingham, and was admitted to Darwin as a graduate member in Category III on 16 October 1968.

I quickly became familiar with the College – taking full advantage of all its facilities. After life in a large civic university, where days were spent between attending lectures, practicals and working in the university library with very little time to interact with colleagues from other disciplines, Darwin was idyllic. I lunched or dined in most days, valuing the opportunity to meet so many interesting people from so many different backgrounds and countries, all passionate about their chosen subjects. The relatively small size of both the Fellowship and graduate members (then around 80) resulted in a real family atmosphere. I also became involved in the activities of the DCSA, becoming Secretary.

I had always wanted to live in College and in May 1969 moved into a room at the end of the top floor of the recently opened Rayne Building, overlooking the river and the picturesque College gardens, where

At a time when my academic subject of economics had, worldwide, not done itself great credit, it was a welcome escape and a great privilege to work with the wider community of the University.

The community that meant most to me, however, was Darwin College. The friendship and support of my immediate colleagues was hugely important. I was blessed with a period of great stability of College officers and staff, and they were unfailingly good to work with. My greatest loss on ceasing to be Master was that of my beautiful office in Newnham Grange. It was always a delight to work in that room, in which Gwen Raverat was born, with its magnificent view of the river and its trees. Although I have lost that, I am indeed fortunate to remain a member of the College community.

## THE MRC CONNECTION
*Darwin, the MRC and Adventures on the Wine Committee*
### Richard Henderson

My adventures at Darwin College span from 1966 to 2012, not quite 50 years. When I was an undergraduate in Edinburgh University Physics Department early in 1966, I decided to move into biophysics and scoured the UK to find a good place for research. After an initial flirtation with King's College, London, I came to Cambridge to visit the MRC Laboratory of Molecular Biology (LMB) which had just been opened (in 1962) on what was then the New Addenbrooke's site. After finding a hive of activity there on a Saturday morning in February, which compared favourably with the less upbeat and relatively deserted

many picnics were subsequently enjoyed. It was from this room that I left for my wedding to David Edmonds in the chapel of Corpus Christi College on 22 August 1970. By then, I was a Fellow of the College, having been elected on 1 January 1970 following my appointment to a demonstratorship in the Botany School. While a Fellow I served on the College Development, Gardens and Buildings Committees as well as the Governing Body and College Council.

I continued to enjoy all the facilities that the College offered until leaving Cambridge for Oxford in 1980 (but retaining my Fellowship until Spring 1981). I particularly valued the friendship and interest shown both to me and to all members by the College Fellowship. Their generosity frequently extended from the College into their homes, where the hospitality of the Fellows and their wives (the majority of Fellows then, as now, were men) was greatly appreciated. Notable for their kindness were Philip McNair, Chester White, Reg Goodwin and Sylvia Fitton

Jackson. The two Masters in post during my time at Darwin – Frank Young and Moses Finley – were also deeply interested in and supportive of all members of the College. I remember sitting next to Frank Young at dinner on both the day that the UK currency became decimalised (when he produced a set of the new coins from his pocket) and the day after the historic moon landing. I also remember with great nostalgia the many formal dinners enjoyed in the new Dining Room, when the tables were initially set as two concentric horseshoes, before diners objected to sitting 'on the corners'. These were often in the company of distinguished guests and even included breakfast with David Attenborough following a Commemoration Dinner.

*Jenny Edmonds (née Gray). In an incident as typical of the age as eyeliner and big earrings, she returned from her honeymoon in 1970 to find that, without consultation, her married name had been adopted throughout College because the Master thought it appropriate.*

## MASTERS AND VICE-MASTERS

### MASTERS

| | |
|---|---|
| 1964–75 | (Sir) Frank George Young |
| 1976–82 | (Sir) Moses Finley |
| 1982–89 | (Sir) Arnold Stanley Vincent Burgen |
| 1989–2000 | (Sir) Geoffrey Ernest Richard Lloyd |
| 2000–12 | William Arthur Brown |
| 2012– | Christine Mary Fowler |

### VICE-MASTERS

| | |
|---|---|
| 1964–75 | Frank George Hayhoe |
| 1975–79 | Gordon de Quetteville Robin |
| 1979–83 | John Arthur (Jack) Jacobs |
| 1983–87 | David Hugh Mellor |
| 1987–90 | Reginald Frederick William Goodwin |
| 1990–97 | Roger George Whitehead |
| 1997–2012 | Andrew Christopher Fabian |
| 2012– | Martin Kenneth Jones |

*The Butler, Paul Jefferies, in the wine cellars of Newnham Grange.*

London laboratory on a Wednesday afternoon, I changed my mind and asked to join the MRC lab, where I have worked ever since, with a brief interlude for three years as a postdoc at Yale. Starting as a PhD student in Cambridge meant having to grapple with the college system, about which little is known in Scotland. So I wrote to another Edinburgh physics graduate, who was a year ahead of me and had joined LMB a year earlier. He kindly sent me a detailed four-page sketch of the strengths and weaknesses of every college in Cambridge. About Darwin, Keith Moffat offered the following insight:

*One other unusual college is Darwin, a purely postgraduate college, very small but expanding fast. The Fellows and students – including my roommate of last year at Edinburgh, Julian Paren – are on an equal footing – none of the high table nonsense. As a result, the food is superb, ridiculously cheap, and the social life on a higher plane altogether. This may change as the College expands – now 20-odd students as against King's, say 450 (90 research), but seems likely to be much the same for a few years yet. If you have a yen to build your own traditions instead of mauling those left by centuries of predecessors, Darwin is worth consideration. It is true though, that the traditional college system is one of the distinguishing features of Cambridge life – which Darwin does not provide. It has one molecular biologist, Ieuan Harris. The rest I know little about.*

In the end I went to Corpus, about which Keith said: 'Corpus Christi has a magnificent postgraduate hostel called Leckhampton, ultra-smooth, full of interesting people and much sought after.'

During my years at LMB, Ieuan Harris, one of the earliest Fellows, would have a drinks party in the Entertaining Room, now renamed the Richard King Room, every November for new people at the Laboratory, so I had some early introduction to Darwin. Ieuan would stand under the portrait of Erasmus Darwin to serve all the drinks in person. Then in 1982, César Milstein asked me to dinner one evening in Darwin. I came along and had a very stimulating and enjoyable evening, talking with Dean Hawkes and others. I thought no more about it until a letter from Moses Finley, the Master in 1982, arrived to say I had been elected as a Fellow, no mention having been made about this by César.

César was a great man, mild, generous and popular, with a tendency to talk for hours and hours. He won the Nobel Prize for Medicine or Physiology in 1984 for his work on the development on monoclonal antibodies (mAbs) with Georges Köhler, becoming the first Darwin Nobel Laureate. His work has led to a multi-billion dollar expansion of the pharmaceutical industry into so-called

**Top left:** *Richard Henderson in the model room at LMB, 1993.*

**Above:** *LMB at the New Addenbrooke's site, 1960s.*

biologicals, with many anti-viral or anti-cancer drugs that have improved the health of millions. Having been founded in 1962 around the work of five Nobel Prize-winners (Sanger, Perutz, Kendrew, Watson and Crick), the MRC Laboratory of Molecular Biology, originally abbreviated to just MRC-Cambridge, but now known as LMB to differentiate it from the many other MRC Units in Cambridge, went on to deliver on its early promise, with more Nobel Prizes in 1980 (Sanger again), 1982 (Klug), 1984 (Milstein), 1997 (Walker), 2002 (Sulston, Horvitz and Brenner) and 2009 (Ramakrishnan), making nine prizes shared among 13 scientists so far, exceeded in Cambridge only by the wealth of physics Nobel Prizes won by scientists at the Cavendish Laboratory. The income to MRC from royalties and share sales from inventions at LMB has been running at £60–70 million per year for many years now, though it will drop sharply when some of the patents run out. Most of this success, along with its economic benefit to the UK, has grown out of César Milstein's scientific work.

Another fond memory of my time at Darwin arose in 1983. Having been brought up in rural Scotland in the small village of Newcastleton, I only encountered wine after reaching Cambridge. At Edinburgh University, we aspired to drink only McEwan's Export brewed in Edinburgh, which was served on draught from 25 identical outlets in the university student union – if there were other offerings, they were difficult to find. So, in 1983, with a friend from my PhD student days at LMB, John Kilmartin, we signed up to a five-week, two-hour evening class in wine appreciation at Parkside Community College. In the exam at the end of the course, John came top of the class (of 25). I did less well, but obviously the news of my new interest reached the hallowed hall of Darwin. A vacancy for the job of Wine Steward and Chairman of the Wine Committee came up, and I was nominated for this position by Ron Laskey, another new Darwin Fellow from LMB. Because of my new enthusiasm I was delighted to take up this heavy responsibility. Our annual budget was about £30,000 and mostly we had to buy inexpensive bottles for under

*César Milstein in the Lab with spinning culture flask used for hybridomas, 1990s.*

£3, since we were catering mainly for those on a research student budget. However, it turned out to be a wise move to retain the Bursar, then Hugh Price, on the wine committee, because whenever there was a good wine available but at a slightly higher price than normal, we were always able to stretch the finances. Being Wine Steward involves going along at lunchtime on two or three days each week to sample all the wines put on show by numerous wine shippers, who come to sell their wares to all the Cambridge colleges during term time. With about 50 occasions like this each year, in each case with 50 or 60 wines on show, a diligent college wine steward could end up tasting between

2,000 and 3,000 different wines each year, accompanied by lunch paid for by the shippers, held in one of a circle of colleges with a big enough room available. Eventually I resigned, as my responsibilities at LMB grew, but I particularly remember one wine that we bought during my time as steward. With help from the Bursar, we acquired 15 cases of 1983 Taylor vintage port, which must be kept for 30 years, so will be ready to drink just in time for the 50th anniversary – and there is plenty of it.

## DARWIN AND NUTRITIONAL SCIENCE – THE EARLY DAYS
### Roger Whitehead

I first learned about Darwin College when I was in Uganda, where I was Director of the UK Medical Research Council Child Nutrition Unit, in 1971. I met Sir Frank Young when he was on a visit to Makerere University for the Inter-Universities Council. About a year later things turned politically difficult in Uganda for the British as a result of President Amin's policies, and I had to close our research unit. I was told that in nine months time I was to be appointed Director of the MRC Dunn Nutrition Unit in Cambridge. Frank immediately arranged dining rights for me at Darwin and, realising that for some time I would be without a proper place of work, said, with astonishing generosity, that I could use his office in the College for any official negotiations I might have before taking up my appointment! Subsequently I was lucky enough to become a Fellow.

During my early days back in the UK Frank was to prove supportive in many other ways. Recognising I needed to establish myself on the UK scene, where I was virtually an unknown in terms of diseases of affluence as opposed to poverty, he arranged membership for me on the councils and governing boards of a number of nutritionally related public bodies. More importantly, during these impossible academic times for their country, the College also admitted two young Ugandan graduate members to work for higher qualifications in nutritional science, Dr Jane Kaggwa and Dr John Kakitahi. Darwin

proved a valuable place for graduates to develop into more rounded nutritional scientists. Although closely linked with physiology and biochemistry it is important that nutritionists develop an appreciation of a range of other associated disciplines, including medicine, sociology and agriculture. The multi-disciplinary atmosphere of Darwin encouraged this in a way no specialised laboratory could. The Dunn's overseas research programme switched to The Gambia in West Africa, and this broader experience among a series of subsequent graduate members was able to develop under the influence of Darwin.

There is another link between Africa and Darwin Masters. Towards the end of Moses Finley's term of office I heard that Sir Arnold Burgen, Director of the National Institute for Medical Research and current Foreign Secretary and Vice-President of the Royal Society, was about to leave his Medical Research Council post and return to Cambridge. I was asked to explore if he might have any interest in Darwin College. My opportunity occurred when Arnold was asked to inspect our nutritional research programme in the isolated rural village of Keneba in The Gambia. During a 'relatively' informal evening gathering in Ann and Andrew Prentice's accommodation there, Arnold was understandably keen to quiz me primarily about the tropical research programme, but (I fear to his initial annoyance) I kept on steering the conversation back to Darwin and to the fact we were beginning the search process for a new Master. He must have realised there had to be method in my madness for he suddenly said that of all the colleges in Cambridge being part of Darwin would suit him the most. I reported back to the Chairman of the Search Committee and the rest is history.

## CESAR MILSTEIN'S ROLE IN BRINGING THE CHARLES DARWIN CHAIR TO DARWIN
### Ron Laskey

When I was appointed to the Charles Darwin Chair of Animal Embryology in 1981/2, several of the more traditional colleges approached me, tentatively expressing

## ELIZABETH BLACKBURN

*Elizabeth Blackburn in Cambridge to receive her honorary doctorate at the Senate House in 2009.*

Professor Elizabeth Blackburn came to Darwin to study for a PhD in 1971. By the time she left Darwin and LMB for postdoctoral research at Yale she had begun her research into telomeres which was to open up important new avenues for cancer research. Together with her then student Carol Greider she discovered an enzyme, telomerase, which plays a key role in the regulation of cell division and ageing. It is for this discovery that she, Carol Greider and their colleague Jack Szostak were awarded the Nobel Prize in Physiology or Medicine in 2009. Elizabeth Blackburn has also won the Bristol-Myers Squibb Award for Distinguished Achievement in Cancer Research, the American Cancer Society Medal of Honor and the L'Oréal UNESCO Award for Women in Science. She is currently Professor in Biology and Physiology at the University of California, San Francisco.

interest in offering me a college Fellowship. Some of these enquiries caused apprehension. The first initiative was an invitation to a college feast, and I realised to my horror that I had left it too late to iron my remarkably crumpled dress shirt if I was to get to the feast on time. One of the traditional features of this feast was that wives of certain guests and fellows dined with the Master's wife in the lodge separately from the main feast, to be reunited with their spouses after the meal. It was then that I found myself caught in the crossfire between Lady X and Lady Y over how they managed to get the correct level of starch into their husband's dress shirts, and Lady X was extolling the virtues of a little laundry near Eton, which knew just how much starch to put in a dress shirt. My chest crumpled still further as this conversation proceeded.

**Left:** *Ron Laskey's* Selected Songs for Cynical Scientists.

**Below:** *Ron Laskey playing his guitar in the Old Library with former Research Fellow Dr Sarah Main and Sally Hames on flute.*

In contrast, I knew Darwin College from our first few years in Cambridge. My wife, Ann, had been a member of Darwin as a consequence of having done her doctorate in our sister college at Oxford, Wolfson, and therefore I dined in Darwin as Ann's guest between 1973 and 1975. I liked the atmosphere in Darwin and immediately felt at home there, and thought Darwin would be a perfect match for the Charles Darwin Chair. However, I did not know any Fellows of Darwin nor did I know whether it would be appropriate to approach a college to ask if they might be interested in a Professorial Fellow whose chair bore the same name as the college. So I suffered in silence and grew increasingly apprehensive as the traditional colleges gradually expressed increased interest.

But then I had an unforgettable conversation. I was working at the MRC Laboratory of Molecular Biology (LMB) at the time, and at one lunch César Milstein asked if I had a moment to spare and could we talk after lunch. I had an enormous respect for César, who was head of one of the divisions at LMB, and who had invented monoclonal antibodies. However, I had no idea why César wanted to talk to me. After lunch I duly joined César in his office, but 15 minutes later I still had no idea why he wanted to talk to me. César was a thoughtful and contemplative individual, and a large part of each sentence was the monosyllable 'errrr' which punctuated every clause. However, this conversation had even more 'errrrs' than usual for César, as he repeatedly debated with himself why I may or may not be interested in 'errrr'. I still had no clue as to the subject of this lengthy debate. Fifteen minutes in I realised the subject was Fellowship of a college, but I still had no idea of which college, as I did not know which college César belonged to. A further five minutes of debate followed, ending in the word 'Darwin' at which I shouted, 'Yes!' This was not enough to convince César, who continued to debate the advantages and disadvantages of Darwin compared to a more traditional college, and I had to reassure him that I really meant 'yes'. I did know Darwin; I had thought about it and knew for sure that Darwin was my preferred college.

*Darwin College trophy cabinet, with some of César Milstein's awards.*

Becoming a Fellow of Darwin had another unexpected benefit. César had to walk four miles a day for medical reasons. As we both lived near Addenbrooke's, he suggested we walk back from Darwin together after Governing Body meetings, with me pushing my bike as we went. The conversation on those walks was always entertaining and interesting, and it was a pleasure to dedicate my Darwin College lecture in 2012 to César's memory. After César's death in 2002 we continued to meet Celia, who became a firm favourite with all the family. So when our son married a Chilean bride she immediately found a kindred spirit in Celia who, like César, was Argentinian.

Without doubt César was one of the most popular of Darwin's Fellows and, as the glass case in the Richard King Room illustrates, he was unquestionably the most distinguished of Darwin's Fellowship to date. Among his numerous medals is the Nobel Prize for Physiology or Medicine, and his inventions have given rise to a multi-billion-dollar industry. César's invention of monoclonal antibodies has had an enormous impact on human health, and it still has even greater promise for further major improvements. It's now over 30 years since César recruited me to Darwin and I shall remain eternally grateful to him.

# DOMESTIC AFFAIRS AND THE DEANERY

*Every Darwin student, if only on arrival and departure, has dealings with the Deanery. (The Dean, for those unfamiliar with the College, fills the function of Senior Tutor, and hence dean of discipline, when necessary. The chapel, deliberately absent, requires no dean.)*

*The first Dean of Darwin was Professor Graham Hough, a man of infinite wit as well as being a distinguished academic and poet. He came to us from Christ's and was one of relatively few Fellows at that time with extensive experience of collegiate activity, but perhaps not a man on whose shoulder one would be encouraged to cry. His tenure, at his own request, was short. He was succeeded by Philip McNair.*

ELG

## Philip McNair

When I became Dean of Darwin in 1965, our graduate members could be counted on the buttons of one waistcoat; but we were in the growing business and rapidly increased from year to year, so that when I quit the post in 1969 we numbered about 120. This was because we enjoyed a spreading popularity at home and abroad, especially in the USA. Even before we opened our doors we had decided to use the term 'Dean' rather than 'Senior Tutor' so that it would be better understood across the Atlantic, and it was not long before applications began to

abound, so much so that quite early in our history we felt obliged to limit our intake of Americans to ten per cent of our admissions in any one year to be fair to other nations.

Those early days and years were exhilaratingly great. We were a pioneering liberal academic society with free and easy attitudes, and we enjoyed a sense of liberation from outworn conventions and meaningless shibboleths. We made up our own rules as we went along. We used to joke that our only fixed prohibition was 'Thou shalt not pick the flowers in the College garden'. We opted for a Latin grace but no chapel. Later, as we began to multiply in the biblical sense, and children fed in our Dining Hall, our egalitarian ethos was encapsulated by the observation

*Left: Philip McNair, Dean 1965–9. He left Darwin in 1974 to become Serena Professor of Italian at Birmingham University.*

*Opposite: The College site, early 1960s, showing the kitchen garden.*

## FRANCISCO GUERRA Y RULLAN

When I was elected Chairman of DCSA around 1973–4, I could not imagine the kinds of issues and challenges I would face; after all, I had come from the Garden Committee, which was a most enjoyable and relaxed position.

Most of the dialogue between the College and students went through the Dean, Dr Goodwin, and the Bursar, Brigadier Crosthwait. The issues were of the utmost importance: objections from the Bursar to multiple occupation of rooms at the Rayne Building and the Old Granary based on violations of fire regulations, and the Dean's concerns about a female French student walking through the corridors in a negligée. I remember few other issues, except for objections from Muslim students about Christian promotional posters in the ground-floor windows of the Rayne Building facing Silver Street, and the need for improved laundry facilities.

Jaroszewicz, the Butler, and the kitchen staff were always interested in our opinion of the quality of the food. On one occasion we organised a weekend garden party at Darwin for which the chef specially prepared a vichyssoise; the soup was not spectacular but the effort was appreciated. Jaros, as everyone called him, had a military-like figure and always announced dinner with pride. He never missed the opportunity to talk about

Poland, including stories from World War II. Jaros showed me how to pour six or seven glasses out of a bottle of wine and supplied with elegance the necessary paraphernalia for several wine tastings we had at Darwin.

Dr Sylvia Fitton Jackson, the Associate Dean, is the person I remember best and with great affection; I never saw her without a smile on her face. She was concerned – in both senses – with receiving new graduate members, particularly foreign ones, to Darwin College, helping us to understand the context and culture and to find our way around successfully. She always remained vigilant about our wellbeing; I knew of several occasions when she had to face difficult situations with students collapsing due to academic pressure, including suicide attempts. My best memory of Sylvia is the day she arrived for formal dinner with her gown – originally black, but by then in green tones – and a wig that constantly changed positions, a situation she described with hilarity. I also remember the various occasions when she invited new graduate members for dinner at her house south of Cambridge, driving as fast as she could in her Jaguar; she served excellent meals and kept what I called her 'vintage gravy' – 'solera' in Spanish – dated, she said, from her student years.

that we had high chairs but no high table. We were a singularly happy community.

The greatest excitement in those early years came in November 1965, when we admitted the first woman, making our graduate members the earliest mixed student body in the history of Cambridge University. (The lucky lady was Jill Sutton, a medic from Somerville College, Oxford.) Lord, how my telephone rang that night! The older women's colleges were not amused. One call came from the Registrary: 'We have been looking into your charter, and can find nothing about admitting women'. 'No', I replied, 'but you will find nothing against it.' And that was the truth: unlike all the older

male colleges, which were restricted by statute to admitting only men, we were free to embrace both sexes. It was probably the best thing we ever did in the last half-century.

Before that year was out, we had admitted our second woman, a fascinating green-eyed Catalan from Barcelona, Helena Valenti y Petit (1940–90), novelist and poet, who inter alia wrote *L'amor adult* (1977) and *D'esqueña al mar* (1991). Since then we have never looked back – and now our Master herself is one of those choice admissions from our salad days.

But there was a downside to our liberated society. One day Mrs P., the bedder who did for the Old Granary, came

## DAPHNE FIELDING DRABBLE

Darwin has always had a special place in my heart. When I first walked into the College in May 1966 I already had a degree in zoology from Oxford and was working at the Natural History Museum in London. But I had decided to change course. On that May evening, I met Julian Paren, John Clarke and J. Patrick Parrinder, three of the original graduate members. We went to the Granta pub and drank a lot of beer. I was then invited to meet the Dean at 9am the next day.

I went up to the Dean's (Dr Philip McNair's) office in fear and trepidation wearing a Laura Ashley frock. He asked: 'Have you read *Period Piece*?'

'Yes,' I replied. 'That's why I want to come here.'

He said: 'Then you can come if you can get a place at the medical school.'

After successful interviews with Professors Boyd and Hayhoe, I was in! Wonderful! They said I was to start in the Long Vac term to do four terms of anatomical dissection. Fine by me. I had time to give my notice and have some annual leave.

I very much enjoyed the Long Vac term. There were still only 12 Fellows and 18 graduate members. We dined in the Darwin family dining room at the family table; Jaros (Aleksander Jaroszewicz), the Butler, looked after me. We drank coffee in the original Parlour (now the Reading Room) with doors to the garden with the Darwin copy of the Wedgwood Portland vase in pride of place. In 1966 the only student rooms were in the Old Granary, occupied by Fr Shea and five other men – so not suitable for girls. In October that year the dining room and Parlour moved into the Hermitage.

At the beginning of the new term at the end of September I was called to the Dean's office. He said: 'There is a problem; the new Registry says we should not have admitted you. The MB is not a postgraduate degree. We think it is. We want you to stay and will arrange it.'

Philip McNair and Dr Reginald Goodwin did just that.

The Dean, as Praelector, presented me for my MA – the first girl to be presented by a man, which was quite exciting. At lunch in College beforehand John Oates, later University Deputy Librarian, threatened to non placet it. Jaros the Butler and a University bulldog promised to thwart him. I felt very special. All went well.

Dr Chester White helped all the way. I was able to do anatomy and physiology in one year, then spent my second year doing pharmacology and pathology.

They had said Addenbrooke's Hospital would be taking medical students, but it didn't until later; so I went to St George's in London.

I have loved watching the College grow and feel honoured to have been one of the earliest students.

round to tell me that a third leg had fallen off one of the beds in her care, and that rumours were spreading through the town: attractive young women had been seen arriving at the door with their suitcases and had taken up illicit residence in the building. Whatever my own liberal and permissive sentiments may have been in those Swinging Sixties, I was put under pressure by the Master and, in particular, the Bursar, Bill Stuart-Clark, to take drastic action, so I carpeted the main offenders and read them the riot act.

In our innocence when the College began, we thought that graduates would have fewer problems than undergraduates, but we were soon disabused. Every term bred fresh challenges and predicaments. Examples include one brilliant but unstable student who seemed to have it in for me, as the College's disciplinary authority, and accused me of being one of the Great Train Robbers (which was considerably exaggerated). She also wrote letters to the World Health Organization saying 'Our Dean lectures on Dante's Hell, and that's where he ought to be!' (They sent me copies.) And then there was another disturbed member, who told me that her psychiatrist had advised her to take a lover, and that I was the chosen one. I was not flattered.

But of course there was a very positive side to being Dean, and for every disturbed genius in the College there were at least 20 others acutely lucid and sane. Ironically enough, despite our secular stance, the greatest influence for good was a young Canadian Catholic priest called Bill Shea, who had entered Trinity College in October 1965 but was so badgered by people seeking his spiritual counsel that he agreed to transfer to Darwin to get some peace. Therefore that December I gave him the best billet in the Old Granary, with a balcony over the river, where breakfast crumbs dropped straight into the water. He and I soon developed a profitable working arrangement: early each morning, after celebrating Mass for some nuns in Grange Road, Bill would come to my room and discuss the moral problems of the day. The College and I owe him a great deal for his balanced wisdom and informed good sense.

Later, after he had left the priesthood, he met a charming Swiss barrister called Evelyn at a party in Darwin, and I had the privilege of marrying them in May 1970 near Lucerne in Switzerland.

During the whole of my term of office, the post of Dean was unpaid, nor would I have accepted any money for it; but I received an entertainment allowance which my wife and I more than spent in inviting graduate members to parties in our house in the Huntingdon Road.

The apex of my modest academic career came when the Master, Sir Frank Young, asked me to deputise for him at the Colleges Committee, made up entirely of Heads of Houses, at a meeting in Pembroke College. Since then it has been downhill all the way.

Being Dean of Darwin was by far the most exciting and worthwhile job that I have ever done in my life, and certainly the most demanding. I dearly loved the work (which I combined with my faculty lectureship, holding supervisions in the Deanery), and was often at my post from 7.15am to near midnight. Why did I quit? I could gladly have done it forever, but my treasured wife warned me that I was seriously overworking and that she had no desire to attend my funeral.

*Philip McNair's successor was Reg Goodwin, whose tenure extended from 1969 to 1983. His reign was marked by, among other things, the spectacular parties, dances even, that he and Joan held at their house in Madingley, certainly not covered by whatever meagre entertainment allowance then existed. It was in his time that a Christmas party for the children of graduate members came into being, with a present for every child attending and, of course, the Dean as Father Christmas. Joan vied with Ruth Young, and also with the Associate Dean, Dr Sylvia Fitton Jackson, in mothering those in need of it. Mothering competition was rife, and all of it much appreciated. Also active in the mothering lists was Daphne Angus, Dean's secretary from 1974 to 1984, whose smiling face welcomed many into the Deanery.*

*Although the post of Associate Dean was originally assumed to require a female officer (the assumption, clearly, being that the Dean would be male) it is not to be supposed that all problems are gender related, or are dealt with as*

*Peter Gathercole, Dean 1983–7, at a party in the College gardens.*

*Bob Sloss, Dean 1987–94.*

*such, and the current ordinances accordingly state that: 'At least one of the Dean, the Deputy Dean and Associate Dean shall be a man and at least one a woman.' Strangely enough no variation of the original distribution of genders has yet been achieved.*

*Reg was followed by Peter Gathercole (1983–7) and he in turn by Bob Sloss (1987–94), whose infinite fund of anecdotes cheered many a meeting. Both Peter and Bob had retired from their University posts on becoming Dean and were always happy to talk and to entertain, in every possible sense.*

*Bob was succeeded by the present Dean, Leo Howe, still in his University post and confronted with a far larger student body.*

ELG

### Leo Howe

One day in 1988 Sir Arnold Burgen, then Master, cornered me in the central corridor (literally, as he backed me against a wall so I couldn't escape) and said: 'You would like to be Deputy Dean, wouldn't you?' I could hardly say no. So began a career of six years as Deputy Dean and, so far, 18 years as Dean.

During this time the University and the College have seen many changes. As far as Darwin is concerned the most significant change has been the rapidly increasing significance, and numbers, of postgraduate students. In the 1980s postgraduates made up about 15 per cent of the student population; today they are more than 35 per cent, and the proportion continues to grow. As a consequence the importance of the graduate colleges is now widely recognised throughout the University, as is the Graduate Tutors' Committee (the inter-collegiate body that oversees graduate affairs), which back then was a little-known and unregarded talking shop.

The doubling of numbers within Darwin means that the College boasts the largest body of graduate members (over 700) in the University. It has been my job,

## BURSARS AND DEANS

### BURSARS

| | |
|---|---|
| 1964–70 | Arthur Campbell (Bill) Stuart-Clark |
| 1970–81 | Michael Leland Crosthwait |
| 1981–94 | Hugh Casburn Price |
| 1994–2001 | Andrew Robert Thompson |
| 2001– | Peter John Brindle |

### DEPUTY BURSARS

| | |
|---|---|
| 1965–8 | John Smart |

### DOMESTIC BURSARS

| | |
|---|---|
| 2012– | Matthew Edwards |

### DEANS

| | |
|---|---|
| 1965 | Graham Goulder Hough |
| 1965–9 | Philip Murray Jourdan McNair |
| 1969–83 | Reginald Frederick William Goodwin |
| 1983–7 | Peter William Gathercole |
| 1987–94 | Robert Sloss |
| | on leave Oct 91–Apr 92, Leo Howe (Acting Dean) |
| 1994– | Leopold Eftimios Anagnostis Howe |
| **Michaelmas 1995, Michaelmas 1998** | Mohammad Munawar Chaudhri (Acting Dean) |
| **Michaelmas 2002** | Matthew Jones (Acting Dean) |
| **Lent 2003** | Margaret Cone (Acting Dean) |

### DEPUTY DEANS

| | |
|---|---|
| 1971–3 | Robert Borland |
| 1981–3 | Peter William Gathercole |
| 1984–6 | Robert Sloss |
| 1986–7 | Harold Frank Woodhouse |
| 1988–90 | Harshad Kumar Dharamshi Hansraj Bhadeshia |
| 1990–4 | Leopold Eftimios Anagnostis Howe |
| 1994–2001 | Mohammad Munawar Chaudhri |
| **Michaelmas 1998, Lent 2000** | John Robert Cooper (Acting Deputy Dean) |
| **Easter 2000** | Matthew Russell Jones (Acting Deputy Dean) |
| 2001– | Matthew Russell Jones |
| 2002–3 | J.H. Swenson-Wright (Acting Deputy Dean) |

and privilege, with many others, to help make Darwin a vibrant, forward-looking and intellectually stimulating place which students want to be a part of. While without doubt the College has been successful in this, the growth in student numbers has increased the pressures on resources. In the Deanery, for example, new policies originating from the University (computerised student information systems, online application forms) and the national government (data protection and freedom of information acts, immigration acts, etc.) means that our work is now more onerous, complicated and time-consuming. Moreover, because the College is exposed to world events, since we attract applicants from over 150 different countries, we are also buffeted by economic turmoil and conflict in places well beyond Europe. We now have far fewer applicants from African states and a great many more from China; we faced difficulty helping students afflicted by the Southeast Asian monetary crisis of the late 1990s; and today we shall have to meet the challenge of some southern European governments slashing grants, with little warning, to their students who come to Darwin.

When I became Dean in 1994 the retiring Dean, Bob Sloss, gave me a piece of advice which I have always found helpful. He said that if everybody liked me or nobody liked me, then I was surely doing a bad job. What he meant was that the Dean has sometimes to make tough decisions which are likely to alienate some students. However much I might have sympathy for a particular student's situation I may have to say 'no' to their request

## SHIGEKO TANAKA

Ryozo and I arrived in Cambridge in the autumn of 1973. As there was no accommodation for a family at Darwin we rented a terraced house in Chesterton. Our morning routine was dropping the elder daughter at the Perse School for Girls, the younger one at the Byron House, parking the car at the Faculty of Oriental Studies where I taught Japanese as a supervisor, and Ryozo attended lectures in Linguistics as a research student. Though he had read English literature and was teaching English as an associate professor at Keio University in Japan, he chose a new subject as a research student.

At Darwin, Dr Reginald Goodwin, the then Dean, and his wife Joan looked after us and gave us various opportunities to meet people at formal dinners. Joan encouraged me to give a talk at a ladies' gathering held at their house about Japanese life and culture, where I played Koto music in our national costume.

One year passed too quickly and Ryozo was allowed by his university to extend his sabbatical leave for another year. He went back to his own subject, Evelyn Waugh, and also started visiting country houses to understand further the background to his novels. Most of our weekends were spent visiting country houses, which became his life-long subject, while I was attracted by their collections of Oriental ceramics on which I began research, and I now write articles on my findings in both languages.

After that first two-year stay in Cambridge we came back to Britain every summer to visit country houses. Ryozo started writing books on them in Japanese and is acknowledged as one of the first Japanese to introduce British country houses to Japan, his books having encouraged Japanese tourists to visit them in groups or individually.

We had two more sabbatical stays at Darwin by ourselves, when he was given a room in the College, where we shared not only the room but also the gown which I wore at Wolfson, whose formal hall was held on another day of the week. We enjoyed the privilege of taking most of our meals in the College hall, where we met much younger members from other parts of the world and eminent dons from other colleges who gave us further opportunities of meeting people who helped our research. The Goodwins' friendship extended as far as our daughters and granddaughter. Professor Sir Geoffrey Lloyd and his wife Ji spent one morning from their tight schedule in Tokyo walking with us in the Imperial Palace garden, and Ji introduced us to her sister, who visited Tokyo and invited us to her villa in France. A student from Turkey gave us not only some advice but small change in case we failed to exchange money at the airport when we visited Istanbul. Some Darwinians have become our life-long family friends. Although sadly Ryozo died in July 2010, Darwin is our second home and I would like to welcome people from Darwin when they visit Tokyo.

*Reg Goodwin, Dean 1969–83.*

in order to maintain equity across students and not to set precedents which I would later regret. Being able to help students with their financial, academic and personal problems is the pleasing side to this delicate equation.

One of the issues that has grieved me most, because I am usually powerless to make a difference, is the fact that every year some three to four students come to tell me of problematic relations with their supervisors. Sometimes this eventuates in a change of supervisor, a change of department, or even a change of university. But one thing is common to most of these cases, and that is that the student usually has to live with uncertainty and anxiety for up to six months as new arrangements are made.

My job has also had some amusing moments. I have a vivid memory of a Greek student coming into my office one day apoplectic with rage, the veins in his neck almost at bursting point, and shouting at me incoherently. He accused me of being a Stalinist, and of spying on the students for my own devious purposes. It gradually became clear that he was complaining about the installation of CCTV cameras in the bar area, for which he assumed I was responsible, and he equated this with the period when the colonels ran a dictatorship in Greece. I assured him I had nothing to do with it, and later discovered that it was the Student Bar Committee which had put the cameras in place to deter further theft of the replacement disco loudspeakers which had recently been stolen. He sheepishly, though reluctantly, later apologised. Another student I well remember, called Rocco and hailing from an Italian American family, was a most likeable and endearing character – until he had a drink. He enjoyed going to discos in the town, having a few drinks and then getting into a fight with almost anyone who would oblige him. Several days later, sober and a bit worse for wear, he would meekly come to seek forgiveness in such a personable way that I could only smile. On one occasion we found him on the roof of the main building, drunk and naked, in the middle of the night.

In closing I want to pay tribute to the approximately 5,000 students who have passed through the College while I have been Dean. With incredibly few exceptions these students have been dedicated, determined, mature and a real pleasure to work with.

## A LODGE WITH A VIEW
### Jack Hicks (Porter 1969–82)
*– reproduced from the 25th Anniversary Magazine*
I remember it well. The Rayne Building was just completed; some members were in residence, but not all the rooms were full, as the College roll was then around the 40s in number. I arrived at College to start work at 5pm, wondering what my new job was to hold for me on this my first day. In the lodge I met a lovely girl, a part-time office worker, who showed me the telephone keyboard and told me where the various offices were, and so on – and she left. Everyone employed by the College was part-time, apart from the chef and the Butler and his assistant. There was just me, all alone in a strange college, with no instructions, not knowing what

*Jack Hicks, Porter, with Jaros (Aleksander Jaroszewicz), Butler.*

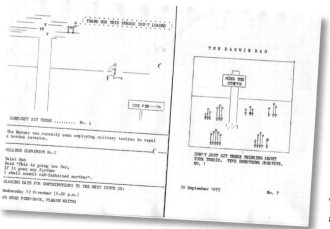

*Two* Darwin Rag *covers, 1975.*

was expected of me and no-one to ask. Later the chef arrived – we had been army friends in war-time – and he showed me up and down the staircases. At seven o'clock the Assistant Butler came and gave me a bunch of keys saying, 'You will need these to lock up and set the alarms.' That was it. (It was very close to being my last day also.) One evening the Master dined and called in to see me. After a long chat he said, 'Well, we are all at a loss about this side of things, and must leave it to you to find out and to do it your way.' From then on, like Topsy, things just grew and grew.

Although in the early days of the College the membership was small, they were a very social society: they mixed very well, ran and organised parties and, although there was no bar, they subscribed together to get beer and spirits, which were kept in a large wooden box and opened for members' benefit at about 10pm, when they returned from the cinema or what have you. From there on things developed to a proper bar when the staff toilets and staff-room were requisitioned. Dances were arranged about four or five times a year, and were kept well under control, and were highly successful and very enjoyable.

I remember also the things that went wrong: the boilers breaking down, especially on a feast night, sewers overflowing, showers and toilets getting blocked, the roofs overflowing in storms, flooding the cellars and fusing the electrics. Also being called from home by the police because the burglar alarms had tripped because of a drop in voltage. But I loved it all. It was only through the knowledge, help and expertise of the Bursar, Brigadier Mike Crosthwait, that many of these problems were overcome. Little do many members appreciate all the things he did for Darwin behind the scenes, unseen, unsung and unthanked.

Over all, my time as Darwin's Head Porter was one of the happiest periods of my life. I met and came to know many lovely people: the whole Fellowship were kind, friendly and civil towards me, especially Sir Frank and Sir Moses and their ladies. Before he retired Sir Frank had one little ritual: whenever he entertained a guest to dinner he would always introduce me to him. He would then say to his guest, 'You know. Jack practically runs the College for me. Isn't that so. Jack?' I would reply, 'Well, sometimes I have a little help from you and the Bursar.' This made him chuckle, and then he would go to dine in good humour.

## Cliff Pennick (Porter, retired 14 December 2012)

Things I will miss:

- The rare appearance of a kingfisher on the river.
- The proud swans displaying their cygnets for the first time.
- Taking the Bursar 'a nice cup of tea' as he laboured into the night. Out of term it seemed that we were the only people working.
- Quiet, late-night chats with tearful girls who had split up with their boyfriends – or just missed their mum.
- Beautiful clothes worn by people at Formal Hall and, of course, the May Ball, and the telephone calls for taxis for the older members who had had a little too much port.
- The friendliness of the chefs and the attention to detail shown by the excellent Butlers.
- Above all, though, it will be the students. Who are the nicest students? That's an easy one. It's got to be the Brazilians – lovely people!

## EVELYNE HANQUART TURNER

I came up in October 1971 on a one-year British Council scholarship to research for my French *doctorat d'état*, a monstrosity which has now been abolished but which, at the time was a necessary condition to ever becoming a university professor. Since my subject was 'E.M. Forster as a humanist', the British Council thought fit to send me to Cambridge. Darwin had been chosen for me and Graham Hough was to be my supervisor. In those far-off days the College was still fairly small but already quite international, though about half the graduate members were British. When I arrived, a few days after the beginning of full term I was immediately thrown into the swing of things, with a sherry party in the room of Sylvia Fitton Jackson, who just as speedily introduced me to Gunther Handl, an Austrian student whom she charged to show me around all the useful bits of College and the various protocols of signing in for dinner, wearing a gown at the right times so as not to incur Jaros's wrath, and of course the bar as the most likely place to make new acquaintances.

I followed Gunther and his advice and soon met many people, who became and have remained good friends. The people I spent most time with during the year were Harlan Cohen; Geta Dumitriu; Franca Losi; Piero Boitani; Gianni Vagi; Tania Croft-Murray; Rob Backus, who more often than not was to be seen mending the punts or *The Griffin* by the Old Granary; Ian Clifton-Everest and his future wife Clotilde, who introduced us to fado; Janet Stephenson; Neil Mulvie; Rob Wallace (now Wallach); and of course the three other Darwinians with whom I shared the house at 47 Granchester Street: Jennifer Fitzgerald, Ian McIvor and Robert Moškovič. For someone coming from the anonymity of the crowded Sorbonne it was such a marvellous change.

But what seemed even more remarkable to me was the attention, the kindness and the genuine interest shown by the Fellows beyond the call of duty. I am eternally grateful, for instance, to John Oates (**left**), who transformed after-dinner small talk typical of the beginning of term into a decisive opportunity which, I am not exaggerating, effected a fundamental change in my research and my professional life; when he heard that I was working on E.M. Forster, he told me that the novelist's papers had just been sorted out at King's and could now be accessible. Would I like to see them? He would introduce me to his colleague, Tim Munby, and no doubt access would be granted. A completely new horizon in research was revealing itself to my incredulous imagination. Sure enough, the following week, after being interviewed by Tim Munby, I was sitting in King's College Library with the first of Forster's manuscripts, in the large bay window facing Cripps Building and the chapel in the distance. I was hardly to be found elsewhere for months! I was the first ordinary scholar to read them.

From this reading my very first research paper emerged, and Graham Hough himself wrote to the editor of *Notes and Queries* on my behalf. The paper was accepted. The supervisions either in his College room or at the White Cottage in Grantchester were unfailingly made less daunting by a good glass of sherry followed by lunch in Hall or at the Green Man. I had never been taught in such a civilised way.

I also fondly remember reading sessions in the College Library on a winter Saturday afternoon, several of us sitting at Talleyrand's table, and taking a well-deserved tea break at Fitzbillie's, whose Chelsea buns, recommended by Fisher Dilke, were much appreciated, or going to Lordsbridge Farm to ride with Helen McFie, who doubled as a champion rower.

### Derek Scott (Head Porter)

Since joining Darwin in 2004 as a College Porter, the years have flown by, and many laughs and smiles have been had along the way, and many thanks to Colin who took me under his wing.

Most of the action has been around the very famous Darwin bar and the great students who have left their mark over the years. From students trying to round up seagulls after a night in the bar, to the many great themed bops and May Balls, and, of course, the students who have plunged into the Cam after punting and are standing in the lodge, still with smiles on their faces.

We now have a team of eight porters and the one thing that has never changed is the way the students always make sure we have a good supply of edible treats. Long may it continue.

### FEAST AND FAMINE

It would be tempting, but perhaps too invidious, to draw a graph indicating the quality of meals in Darwin over the last 50 years. High points would be the notorious Mrs Jackson, a cordon bleu, in the early days (1964–7), and the arrival of Ian MacTulloch-Gair in 1988, when we all thought that we had died and gone to the Ritz (or at least Peterhouse). It wasn't that Ian's skills diminished subsequently, just that the deficit on the kitchen account increased. His later days were pretty good too, but not *quite* so spectacular.

Normally really, really good chefs applying for College posts are bound to favour those which have lots of feasts, preferably endowed ones. Ian appeared to be happy to deal with our less spectacular demands. He came from the armed services, from the Catering Corps, and had made a deliberate decision to cater for the 'other ranks', which figures. His predecessor, also from the Catering Corps, had elected to be chef to a General. The said General has our sympathy.

ELG

*Catering staff, 2013.*

### GEORGE GÖMÖRI

During the 1970s I was involved with the Cambridge Poetry Festivals and had the pleasure of getting to know many excellent poets and literati who were invited to participate. In 1974 one of the main guests of the Festival was the Swedish poet Tomas Tranströmer and his Scottish translator, Robin Fulton. Having corresponded with Fulton earlier, I invited both of them for lunch in Darwin. In those days Darwin was not best known for its cuisine and this particular meal certainly was not one of its highlights.

Sitting down to eat, I was horrified when the waiter put down in front of each of us a plate of tinned spaghetti. Tranströmer took a forkful of the spaghetti, put down his fork and calmly announced: 'I am not eating this.' I called the Butler, who removed the offending spaghetti and served my Swedish guest a plateful of boiled potatoes and salad.

At the next meeting of the College's prestigious Meals Committee, of which I was a member, I pleaded with the Kitchen Superintendent, a lady who had previously run a boarding house, never to serve this tinned monstrosity again. Generations of graduaute members coming from around the world to study in Darwin have little idea that it is at least in part Tomas Tranströmer, awarded the Nobel Prize for Literature in 2011, to whom they should be grateful for one of the dramatic improvements of Darwin's kitchen.

## SHAZEEDA ALI

The academic year 1994–5 may be described as 'the year of living globally'. This was my year at Darwin College, where I met someone from almost every country in the world. The exposure significantly broadened my understanding of the international community as I was able to gain insight into the culture and practices of many foreign lands.

The kitchen on my floor was a veritable mini-UN and, certainly, if the problems of this world could be resolved through gastronomic delight and the art of conversation, then we would have discovered the secret to world peace, as mealtime was not simply an opportunity to exchange delicacies but a chance to learn about the customs and ethos of those gathered. It was in that kitchen too that I honed my culinary skills and expanded my repertoire of recipes. Indeed, it seems as if much of my recollections revolve around food, because who could forget the fine cuisine at formal hall, coffee in the Parlour and even fish and chips Friday!

My stint as the editor of the DCSA's student magazine *The River Rat* was exciting, and an important learning experience. It helped to fuel my interest in writing and publishing, a significant part of my life today.

My tiny room on the 3rd floor had a fantastic view of the Cam. As I was not one of the lucky few to have my own en-suite shower, I remember trekking down to the showers on the floor below, at the crack of dawn, with all my bath gear in tow, trying to be first in line for the shower while it was still squeaky clean! Although the use of certain appliances in the room was forbidden, I managed to keep a small toaster on my desk. I remember the night when my burnt toast set off the fire alarm on my floor. I trembled with fear of expulsion as my contraband toaster was sure to be exposed. Imagine my utter relief when my penitent confession to the Porter was simply met with loud laughter absolving me of this guilty secret.

## BENEFACTORS
### Richard King

It was Hugh Fleming, a cardiologist at Papworth Hospital and a Fellow and Emeritus Fellow of Darwin College who once said to me, 'Do you know, Richard, of all the organisations with which I have been associated across the world, I think Darwin College is the most worthwhile.'

Over the years that I have been a Fellow I have come to share that view. I like the College ethos and style. Also, importantly, the sense of purpose and commitment to research-based learning.

I have been fortunate enough to have been able to support the College financially in a number of ways. Nothing grand, like a whole building, but smaller projects that 'needed to be done'. I made it known to the Master and the Bursar that I was happy to leave it to them as to how the money was spent. I did, however, say I was not keen on bricks and boilers. The one exception was, and is, the Darwin College Lecture Series, an opportunity for Darwin to show its intellectual clout in a public shop window.

Largely, I have dribbled money into the College coffers over the years. I was fortunate enough to have created shareholdings in three successful Cambridge-based hi-tech companies with which I was closely involved (I keep rather quiet about the unsuccessful

*A lunch-time seminar in the Richard King Room.*

ones). Transferring shares to Darwin, a charity, is quite an efficient thing to do. I have also, on occasion, transferred small bundles of money that were tied up in savings that had somehow lost their original purpose and were earning pathetically low interest.

I have to admit to being somewhat ambivalent towards giving personal publicity to my benefactions – an odd word. I think I prefer some of its synonyms: supporter, backer, contributor, helper, well-wisher and friend. But whatever word is appropriate, I have been persuaded that, if in some way I might further encourage other people to do similar things, I should do so.

Darwin is by no stretch of the imagination a wealthy Cambridge college. But it has big needs and big ambitions. Many of these can only be funded internally.

For me, it is a pleasure and a privilege to support an organisation built upon significant educational and research capabilities, diversity and intellectual challenge: the 'stuff' of which great postgraduate colleges are made.

## MAX RAYNE

Lord Rayne is a familiar figure to every member of Darwin because of the magnificent portrait of him by Graham Sutherland that dominates the Dining Hall. Fewer will know that the reason it is there is because it was the generosity of Lord Rayne, through the Rayne Foundation, that made the construction of the Hall and of the Rayne Building possible. Some will have encountered Lord Rayne when he attended Commemoration Dinners, which he did every year until too ill to do so. Max Rayne was born in London in 1918 to a family of poor immigrant Jews from Poland. After service in the RAF during the war he returned briefly to the family tailoring business before turning to property development, at which he showed prodigious gifts and made a great fortune. He believed that the money he made should be used for the public good, and his beneficiaries were quite varied. The Sutherland painting was inspired by his deep love of art, which led to both a splendid personal collection, but also to generous support of the National Gallery. He was also a benefactor of the theatre, opera, ballet and architecture, as well as many other activities, notably hospitals, including St Thomas's and the Burns Unit at East Grinstead. He gave freely of his time on committees and was a long-serving Chairman of the Board of the National Theatre. He was also a governor of the Royal Ballet School and played an important role in RADA, the Yehudi Menuhin School and an extraordinary number of other artistic and charitable

*Max Rayne by Graham Sutherland.*

ventures. He was raised to the peerage in 1976 and died in 2003. We at Darwin have every reason to be grateful for his interest in and generosity to the College.

*Arnold Burgen*

### GIFTS TO THE LIBRARY

The College Library has been the beneficiary of two significant gifts: the first was the personal library of Moses Finley, bequeathed to the College on his death in 1986. This is a remarkable collection of books covering society and thought in the world of Ancient Greece and Rome, and provides an important research resource. Perhaps the Library's greatest treasures, however, are the first editions of two extraordinary early medical books, *De Humani*

*Corporis Fabrica* (1543) by Vesalius and the *Opera Quae Extant Omnia* (1645) by Spigelius. The Vesalius is richly illustrated with beautiful and detailed woodcuts by Calcar, a pupil of Titian, while Spigelius represents the final flowering of the golden age of anatomy at Padua. These were given to the College in 1995 by Geoffrey Fisk, who came to study for an MPhil in anthropology in 1990 at the age of 74. He was particularly interested in the morphology of the wrist joint and the heel bone, and was the first clinician to examine bones from burial sites in Upper Egypt from the Duckworth Collection of the Museum of Archaeology and Anthropology. Fisk had been the last house surgeon to Sir Geoffrey Keynes, husband to Margaret Darwin, at St Bartholomew's, which may have influenced his choice of college. A distinguished medical career subsequently led him to the Seamen's Hospital in London, to the Hunterian Chair of the Royal College of Surgeons and, finally, to Darwin.

*Right: Frontispiece from Vesalius,* De Humani Corporis Fabrica.

*Below: A Darwin family reunion in College for the bicentenary of the birth of Charles Robert Darwin, 2009. The extended Darwin family has been very supportive of the College, loaning family treasures, making donations and featuring from time to time as both graduate members and honorary Fellows.*

# THE DARWIN COLLEGE LECTURES AND COLLOQUIA

## EDUCATION AND RESEARCH: THE EARLY YEARS

### Dean Hawkes

I became a Fellow of Darwin in 1976, early in the Mastership of Moses Finley. By then the College was securely established, with nearly 200 graduate members, and was seeking to forge a distinctive identity in the life of the University.

The first step on the path was the creation, in 1976, of a Colloquium Committee, of which I was a member. Chaired by the Master, this was driven along by the enthusiasm of its Secretary, Dr A.F. (Sandy) Robertson. It was felt that a graduate college provided an ideal context for the examination and discussion of issues that did not fall within the scope of departments or faculties, and that this might be achieved through the promotion of interdisciplinary activities. In the years from 1976 to 1979 the Darwin College Colloquium became an important part of College life. Topics discussed included 'Censorship', 'Intelligence', 'Concepts of modern physics', 'Architecture' and 'Crisis in Britain?' Perhaps the most notable event was a series of six meetings on the subject of 'Professors and Professionals'. These explored the diverse relationships that exist between the academic disciplines and professional practices. At each an eminent academic and a practitioner led the debate, and the event received

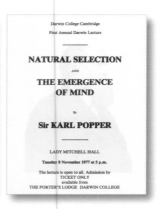
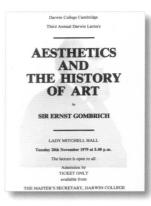

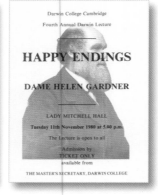

*Above:* The Annual Darwin Lecture, posters for the first four years, 1977–81.

*Opposite:* Darwin College Lecture in Lady Mitchell Hall, January 2013.

national attention in three articles published in the *Times Higher Education Supplement* in the spring of 1978.

In 1977 the College held the first annual Darwin Lecture, delivered on 8 November by Sir Karl Popper, on 'Natural selection and the emergence of mind'. For the first time a Darwin College event brought a full house to the Lady Mitchell Hall. In the following year two lectures were given, the first by Willard Quine, on 'Physical

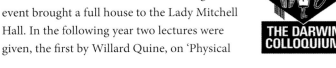

objects', followed by Christian de Duve, on 'The biological revolution'.

In 1979 the Education and Research Committee was established, and was entrusted with the administration of the newly created Education and Research Fund. I was appointed the committee's first Chairman. There were three sub-committees, the Colloquium Committee, the Darwin Lecture Committee and, looking ahead to 1982, the

*Above:* Logo used by the *Times Higher Education Supplement*. *Below:* Christian de Duve (second from right), who gave the Second Annual Darwin Lecture in 1978, with his wife, Moses Finley, the Chancellor, and Sir Alan Cotterell, Vice-Chancellor.

Darwin Centenary Conference Committee. (This is described on p99 of this publication by Hugh Mellor.) The College's academic life was, thereby, given formal expression and substance. That year Sir Ernst Gombrich lectured on 'Aesthetics and the history of the arts'. In the years that followed the lecturers were: Dame Helen Gardner (1980), 'Happy endings'; Freeman Dyson (1981), 'Life in the universe'; Sir Andrew Huxley (1982), 'How far will Darwin take us?'; and Lord Lane (1983), 'Do we get the criminals we deserve?'. In 1984 Alfred Brendel gave a wonderful lecture recital, held at the Music School to accommodate his Steinway grand piano, on, 'Does classical music have to be entirely serious?' The following year the lecturer was Tom Stoppard on 'The less than sacred text'.

In its first year the Education and Research Committee introduced the College Groups. There were initially four groups: Arts, Biological Sciences, Mathematics and Physical Sciences, and Social Sciences. These quickly became established and provided graduate members with a platform upon which they could present their work to a sympathetically critical audience, and laid the ground for the successful lunchtime seminars in Humanities and Social Sciences and the Sciences that continue to the present day.

## THE ORIGIN AND EARLY DEVELOPMENT OF THE DARWIN COLLEGE LECTURE SERIES
### Arnold Burgen

I had a most interesting and enjoyable time as Master from 1982 to 1989 but the most important activity during that period was undoubtedly the start of the Darwin College Lecture Series. The intellectual life of the College since the time of Sir Moses Finley had been enhanced by seminars, conferences and lectures, notably the prestigious Annual Darwin Lecture which was instituted in 1977, but the proposed Lecture Series represented a new activity of great importance.

It was partly inspired by the success of the conference organised by the College to mark the centenary of Charles Darwin's death.

At a meeting of the Governing Body on 5 December 1983 it was decided to set up a new sub-committee of the Education and Research Committee to consider possible future lecture activity. The committee was composed of the Master, Vice-Master (Hugh Mellor), Andrew Fabian, Derek Bendall, Adrian Gill, Paul Ries (who acted as the Secretary) and a graduate member, Donald Smith. Dr Gill departed from the College after the first meeting when the committee was augmented by Peter Gathercole and Philip Johnson-Laird.

The committee discussed several kinds of activity including major conferences, but preferred a series of small symposia or a series of lectures. They noted that Wolfson, our sister college in Oxford, had a successful scheme in which there was a regular lecture each week during one of the terms, and this seemed a useful model to follow. The committee envisaged a set of eight lectures given weekly in one term. It was important that they should be interdisciplinary between the humanities and the sciences and hence needed to be readily understandable by non-specialists, and would be focused around a common theme. They would be known as the Darwin College Lectures and would be published in book form. It was initially proposed that the lectures would be given in the College Hall in Lent Term on Fridays at 5pm, followed by discussion.

The committee then gave thought to topics and, after discussion with colleagues, it was decided to focus on 'Origins', a theme with obvious relevance to the College. Possible topics covered would be the origins of the universe, the solar system, Earth, life, societies, language and institutions. After consultation with the Fellowship for further topics for consideration this format was accepted. Professor Fabian agreed to act as the organiser and to be editor of the publication. Having reported back to the Education and Research Committee and to the Governing Body, agreement was given to go ahead and identify speakers; this was accomplished by May 1985 and the first series was planned for the Lent Term of 1986.

Dr Mellor wrote an introduction to the Series and the list of speakers was as follows:

Martin Rees: The origin of the universe
David W. Hughes: The origin of the solar system
Lynn Margulis: The origin of life
Ilya Prigogne: Origins of complexity
David Pilbeam: The origin of man
John Maynard Smith: Origins of social behaviour
Ernst Gellner: Origins of societies
John Lyons: Origins of language

In the first talk Professor Rees confidently proclaimed that the universe had begun in a Big Bang some 13 billion years ago but without man, who had to wait for a while. As we proceeded through the lectures the time of origin of the subject became progressively more recent and uncertain. For instance, it was very unclear as to when a recognisable man had evolved from a primate and even more unclear as to when he began to make sense out of vocal noise and expletives to create a language.

By the time the speakers had agreed to participate it was realised that the space available in the College Hall might not be adequate and, fortunately, it was possible to book the Lady Mitchell Hall. There had been thoughts about having a discussion after the lecture and, in the event, this was dropped.

So on 16 January 1986 an audience which filled the hall heard the first lecture. The large audience continued throughout the series and it was obvious that it had found a place in the Cambridge calendar and was an unexpectedly great success.

As had been agreed the Cambridge University Press undertook to publish a text of the lectures in which some of the authors could develop the subject beyond what was possible in an hour, and the volume was ably edited

*Roger Whitehead, former Vice-Master, on door duty at the Darwin College Lecture Series, 2012.*

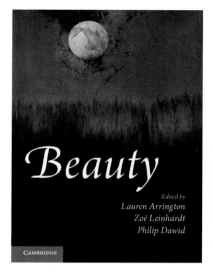 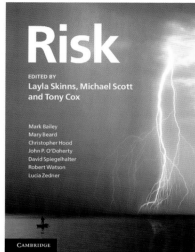 

*Publications from the Darwin College Lecture Series.*

by Professor Fabian. The book sold well and was even translated into Italian and, much later, into Japanese. Many years later podcasts of the lectures were made available on the Web and widely accessed.

The organising committee was so confident of the success of the venture that they had already developed the programme for a second series long before the first lecture was delivered. The subject chosen was 'Man and the Environment', and Professor Ron Laskey undertook its organisation. It was an excellent and prescient choice. Among the subjects covered were human impact on future climates, exhaustible resources, famine, the future of forests and of animal populations, and the observation of the environment from space. An excellent range of topics was thus encompassed, all of which are still vigorously discussed at the present time.

It was clear the Darwin College Lecture Series was a going concern, but I don't I think that anyone would have forecast that they would be as vital and popular after so many years. The Series continues and indeed has not run out of steam. They have become an established part of the Cambridge scene in Lent Term.

## THE EVOLUTION OF THE DARWIN COLLEGE LECTURE SERIES

**Andrew Fabian**

2013 saw the 28th of the Darwin College Lecture Series (DCLS), with over 220 lectures given since 1986. I have been involved in them since the start, organising the first one, 'Origins', the tenth, 'Evolution', the 20th, 'Conflict', the 24th, 'Darwin', and the 27th, 'Life' (the last three jointly with Martin Jones and Willy Brown). For most of that time I have chaired the Education and Research Committee which oversees the Lecture Series.

A book, *The State of the Universe*, from a lecture series in Oxford which took a specific academic discipline each year, acted as a trigger rather than a model for our series. In Darwin we take a topic, usually a single word, that can serve as an umbrella for a wide range of topics. We try hard to cover the physical, biological and social sciences as well as the humanities through separate lectures within a single Series. The interdisciplinarity of the DCLS is a strength, a uniqueness and yet a problem for publication. Cambridge University Press have supported us throughout by publishing each Lecture

*Books from the Darwin College Lecture Series.*

Series but have always told us that booksellers don't know how to market such volumes. Is 'Origins' astronomy (the cover has a galaxy), human evolution (there's also a skull), social science or biology? Personally, I rather like collections of disparate interesting topics, in the same way that reading the book reviews section of a weekend paper is pleasurable as well as informative.

The books of the Series are available online. Much effort has been put into producing high-definition video of the lectures themselves, which can be downloaded from iTunes U, as approaching a million people have already done. We aim to enlist the very best communicators as speakers and that shows by the high quality of the talks. The DCLS has become the largest public lecture series in Cambridge, with typically 300 to 500-plus in attendance. The Series has continued over the last few years thanks to several very generous

donations by Richard and Anne King and there has also been an enormous amount of sustained effort and help given by Fellows and graduate members of the College. At the centre of the communications, the Master's secretaries over the years, Joyce Graham and Janet Gibson, have acted with the attention and enthusiasm necessary for the sometimes fraught activities which make for a successful series.

So who have we had as speakers? Eleven Nobel Prize winners so far, including some of the best, and some of the worst speakers! Martin Rees started the series off with 'The origin of the universe' (we've always been ambitious in scope) and also closed the tenth with 'The evolution of the universe'. Robert May also spoke twice ('Animal population changes' and 'Beauty and truth') and Noam Chomsky did 'Language and mind' to an overflowing lecture hall. Other highlights included:

Stephen Hawking: 'The future of the universe'

Roger Penrose: 'Mathematical intelligence'

Daniel Dennet: 'Intelligence, language and consciousness'

Bridget Riley: 'The artist and colour'

Helena Kennedy: 'Human rights'

Stephen J. Gould: 'Evolution of evolution'

Jared Diamond: 'Evolution of guns and germs'

A.S. Byatt: 'Memory and making of fiction'

Simon Conway-Morris: 'The structure of life'

Baroness Warnock: 'The bioethics of reproduction'

Konrad Spindler: 'The iceman's body'

Neil deGrasse Tyson: 'Powers of ten'

John Conway: 'Power of mathematics'

Alex Jeffreys: 'DNA fingerprinting'

Robert Winston: 'DNA in reproductive medicine'

Brian Greene: 'Superstrings'

Simon Baron-Cohen: 'Sex differences in mind'

Richard Wrangham: 'Why apes and humans kill'

Kate Adie: 'Reporting conflict'

James Jackson: 'Surviving natural disasters'

Marcus du Sautoy: 'Mathematical identity'

Simon Singh: 'Cosmological serendipity'

Richard Leakey: 'Understanding humans'

Steve Jones: 'Why Darwinism is right'

David Speigelhalter: 'Risk and statistics'

Ben Goldacre: 'Risk, science and the media'

Mary Beard: 'Risk and the humanities'

Frank Wilczek: 'Quantum beauty'

A science bias is perhaps a little obvious. But we also have had politicians (Tony Benn, Shirley Williams, Desmond Tutu and Oliver Letwin), memorable performance art in talks by S. Arom ('Senegalese drumming') and Shobana Jeyasingh ('Indian ballet'), and architects (Richard Rogers and Daniel Libeskind).

*Michael Scott speaks at the Darwin College Lecture Series, 2012.*

## LEARNING AT DARWIN: SHERRY AND PORT

Learning comes about in different ways. My first challenge at Cambridge was to further the development of a computer program for the automatic design of three-dimensional roof structures, designed by my supervisor John H. Frazer in the Department of Architecture; the program operated with a 'seed' and a set of instructions to make it grow so as to cover a pre-determined space, each instruction being generated at random with the capability to learn from failed and successful attempts. For an architect's frame of mind, such as mine, this is a straightforward challenge that offered no room for diversions or additional thought.

However, when I discussed this with fellow students and dons at Darwin – particularly philosophers and over a glass of sherry or port – their observations revealed a significant resemblance between the underlying concepts of what I was doing in the automated design process with the way nature performs in the context of Charles Darwin's ideas.

Darwin's ideas led me to attempt to understand the significance of chance occurrences in any design process or even daily decision making; after all, I remain an architect, a designer of strategies social, political, economical and environmental. The concept of 'chance' allowed me to get close to an understanding of how the designer's mind works. Only at Darwin College did I find people sympathetic to these ideas, and one of them was Gerd Buchdahl, a philosopher of science with whom I had the opportunity to talk and learn about György Ligeti, a Hungarian composer whose music we both enjoyed; Ligeti had an interest in fractal geometry and a fascination for machines that do not work properly, so the ticking of random mechanical noises of unreliable machinery occurs in his works. Gerd Buchdahl's comments and suggestions about chance and random events took place before and after dinner in a stochastic fashion since we never planned a meeting, but every time we coincided there was an opportunity to learn something new from him.

When I arrived at Cambridge in late 1971, Hugh Mellor had just published *The Matter of Chance*, but somehow I never approached him to talk about my interest in random-generated hypotheses as a design process strategy, probably because I was not ready to talk about chance events with an expert. Nevertheless, Hugh Mellor was always interested in commenting or pursuing any idea we proposed, whether philosophical or otherwise.

Darwin College also led me to the ideas of Karl Popper. Again, the fantastic power of ideas in one context that can be applied in almost any other context – something that can be learned only in a plural environment. I would no doubt have appreciated meeting Karl Popper, even from a distance, but the time came for me to leave Darwin College and return to my professional life in Mexico; it was a difficult decision, because Cambridge had become an addiction and it was unthinkable for me to leave behind the intense absorbing of knowledge that I had enjoyed in the College and the University.

Nevertheless I managed to survive, finding alternative ways to keep myself up to date in some issues; the internet has satisfied a thirst for knowledge for many, but for me it cannot replace those chance encounters at Darwin College.

In my professional life as a consultant on strategies, competitiveness and territorial intelligence, I'm frequently asked how I build my approach to solving complex challenges successfully, which some people find interesting. My internal response is the mind-set I acquired while at Darwin College; my public response is more elaborate, with a couple of well-chosen references. I did learn many relevant things at Cambridge, but the fundamental change in my mental approach, something that has proved to be essential in my professional and private life, came from those unplanned encounters and conversations over a glass of sherry or port at Darwin College.

*Francisco Guerra y Rullan (1971–8)*

## A BACKBONE OF STEEL

Following a meeting in Florida back in 1993, I returned to Cambridge feeling confused about networks of neurons; a book that I bought on the subject did not help. It was in a disgruntled mood that I went, as I usually do, to Darwin for lunch and started to pontificate on how useless conferences are in communicating information and how books are not what they used to be. Sitting next to me was David MacKay, who turned out to be the saviour. We began to work together and published some 14 articles of unfunded research, stating the notional Darwin College Mathematics and Physical Sciences Group as our affiliation and formally acknowledging the College Education and Research Committee for creating an environment which nurtures learning. David's method has now been implemented in many parts of the world where steel matters, i.e. everywhere!

The meals we have together, the lunch talks in particular, and the fact that I never feel uncomfortable in talking to anyone in College is what I have appreciated the most. Janine Bourriau once 'translated' for me the term representing my favourite crystalline phase in steel, into Egyptian hieroglyphics. Carlos Martin, the cosmologist, corrected some of my mathematics. A rather long lunchtime disagreement with one of the PhD students in Darwin led me to write what is now an influential paper, with the first proof that it would be impossible, even in principle, to build an elevator into space using carbon nanotubes. I did send the paper to NASA, which had invested some $17 million in the project. Incidentally, the paper has a photograph of my sock (and the leg within), but you would have to read it to understand why.

And there are many more stories to tell, including some failures. A group of us in Darwin attempted to create a religion based on principles which could not lead to conflict. The concepts were soon challenged, by astrophysicists, mathematicians, engineers and others. Nevertheless, I take comfort in the fact that to assess religion requires patience, perhaps on the scale of centuries of noisy propagation. Then there were the futile protests in which many Darwinians participated, to persuade Tony Blair to avoid the loss of life that followed in Iraq. My attempts to reverse the ill-advised decision to move the portraits from the Dining Hall into the Old Library were irrationally opposed at the Governing Body. I set a challenge to a few of the sceptical humanities scholars in Darwin to prove me wrong that there is no starvation in the world today, only that created by conflict or dictatorship – they have yet to respond.

And I had an unsatisfactory discussion with a prolific author in Darwin, on whether a textbook is a book and vice versa!

My emphasis here is about the academic excellence that exists in our college. We do not need research councils, financial incentives or top-led directives to work together across the subjects. Darwin has done its magic without intervention. To me this is its seminal achievement, and a surprising one given its youth.

*Harry Bhadeshia PhD 1980, Fellow since 1985*

## PARLOUR TALK

I'm sitting in the Graduate Centre (grad pad) reading an article about quantum physics, and I am wondering why my curiosity remains so keen and positively youthful, as I settle into the 'contented period' of my life. I look across at Darwin College and gain immediate insight as I fondly remember the multiverse of parlour talk in which I had lived for over three years. Coffee times in the Parlour were the highlight of my day. I never quite knew what to expect because the one thing that we all had in common was that we didn't actually have too much in common. We had different nationalities, different ages and different subjects, and it was this mix that made me feel like I had access to the whole intellectual wealth of the world – and I loved it. We pursued truth, and no prisoners were taken. We needed to be explicit, listen very carefully to often beautifully constructed arguments, and most importantly, among friends we learnt to ignore any twinges of ego. It wasn't all about work, however – creativity comes in many guises and I had mine stretched to its limits just trying to keep up with the humour. I fondly remember a friend explaining to us in detail about how he might crash a May Ball. He was going to cleverly circumvent security by building an over-ground tunnel. It's so ridiculous that it still makes me laugh today. The humour was fast and infectious; no wonder Cambridge produces so many comedians. Staying in contact with old friends from Darwin has been a great way to remain young. When we meet up we barely notice the 30 years in between, and I always feel my cognition sharpening in preparation. I can't help thinking that the sophistication of the Parlour played its role. The William Morris wallpaper, soft brown leather sofas, grand chairs, beautiful views of the gardens and river, not to mention those intense glances from the portraits of Darwin and his family, all conspired to provide some of my finest hours.

*Linda Bowns (1983–9)*

## COMING HOME

In 1966 I was about to finish my mathematics degree at Trinity Hall and wondering what to do next. Partly because I thought it might be a route to a good job (well, I did become a career academic), but mostly from sheer inertia, I opted to stay on at Cambridge to take the Diploma in Mathematical Statistics. But at least my inertia stopped short of total paralysis. I had recently learned of the establishment of a brand new college, which was to be restricted to graduate students. Also, it was admitting students of both sexes, and these students were to dine at the same table as, and even eat the same food as, the Fellows. These astounding innovations were unheard of in 750 years of Cambridge history – here was something completely different, surely worth trying out.

So I applied to switch to Darwin College. My suitability was assessed by an unannounced informal visit to my room in Trinity Hall, while I was preparing a particularly smelly lunch, by Charles Darwin himself – as I initially mistook the Dean, Philip McNair, to be. But I passed inspection, and was admitted in October 1966 as one of the second intake of students at Darwin. My arrival brought the total student body to 48 – a good start on the road to the current tally of over 700 graduate members.

After 40 intervening (and not entirely uneventful) years in London, I returned to Darwin in 2007 as a Professorial Fellow. I had naively expected to be the oldest-serving Darwinian, but found myself outranked by several Fellows, including Abe Yoffe and Chester White, who had joined Darwin before me and were still here. And they were

*The Parlour.*

not the only perfectly preserved features of Darwin: the overall look and feel of the place gave me a remarkable, indeed unsettling, sense of timeless continuity.

The Parlour in the Hermitage appeared completely unchanged, with the identical William Morris wallpaper, deep leather armchairs, and portrait of Charles Darwin, all unfaded – or at any rate no more faded than before.

After a while I did notice a few small changes. The main entrance into Newnham Grange had been blocked off, allowing the two rooms on either side to be knocked together to form the 'Old Library'. There was a splendid modern Dining Hall, the Rayne Building for on-site accommodation as well as various off-site student residences, and the Study Centre, for watching the boats and ducks glide by. The College had also spread sideways into existing buildings on Newnham Terrace. But in spite of the increases of both physical size and student numbers, it is remarkable how the College has managed to retain exactly the same feel it had when it was young. Coming back to Darwin has been just like coming home.

*Philip Dawid*

*The bar.*

# THE DARWIN CENTENARY CONFERENCE
*'Evolution of Molecules and Men': The Darwin Centenary Conference, 27 June–2 July 1982*

## Hugh Mellor

In 1982 the College ran what the journal *Science* called 'the most official of the multiplicity of conferences to commemorate the centenary of Darwin's death'. This was a fair verdict, for as Moses Finley said in his Master's Preface to *Evolution from Molecules to Men*, the conference volume edited by Derek Bendall and published by Cambridge University Press in 1983, 'no other conference took so wide-ranging a view of the present state of Darwinism'. That indeed was our intention, for only so, we thought, could we make the occasion worthy of its subject and of the College. Its success depended primarily of course on our galaxy of speakers who, as the papers in the conference volume attest, did Darwin and his legacy proud. The 30 topics listed in the programme *(see p101)* covered everything in the conference title and more: from the evolution of molecules to that of Darwinism itself, and of its implications for ethics and the human and biological sciences. The range and quality of the papers and the standard of discussion in the sessions made this as absorbing and enlightening a conference as I ever expect to attend.

Today the College routinely runs large events, like the Annual Darwin College Lecture Series. But in 1982 organising a conference on this scale seriously taxed a new and none-too-rich graduate college. (To take but one example: the year-round residence of its graduate members prevented Darwin from housing the conference's many eminent external participants.) Fixing the programme, travel and accommodation kept many Darwin staff, Fellows and graduate members busy for months if not years, not least Derek Bendall, the indefatigable editor of the 600-page conference volume, which he got published the very next year. But Moses made helping out the College in these ways feel more like a privilege than a chore. He certainly made me feel that when, walking into lunch in Hall in the spring of 1980, he did me the honour of hi-jacking most of my spare time for the two years it took us to make the conference happen.

The mostly routine and time-consuming preparatory work did, however, present a few unexpectedly interesting challenges. One was coping with the acoustics of our venue, the West Road Concert Hall, which then as now was better suited to music than to speech. Our pre-conference tests showed that most speakers mistakenly felt they needed to raise their voices to be clearly heard, which they didn't: on the contrary, raised voices merely awoke an unhelpful echo from the back of the hall. The solution, we found, was to place a prominent microphone on the lectern – and then turn it (almost) off.

A less serious but more enjoyable challenge was prompted by my remarking, at the opening reception, that I thought the photograph of Charles Darwin on the programme cover cried out for a *Private Eye* speech bubble. This provoked the idea of a competition, which I announced at the first session, the winner's prize being some claret, kindly donated by Jeremy Mynott on behalf of Cambridge University Press. Few of the submitted suggestions were any good, with the easy winner, announced at the closing session, being 'Have you read my book?'. It's a pity, though, that the only one *Private Eye* might actually have published – 'Fuck the fittest!' – wasn't put to me by its author, Tim Clutton-Brock, now Prince Philip Professor of Ethology and Evolutionary Biology, until the post-conference party. But even if it never made *Private Eye*, it wasn't wasted: Pat Bateson, Emeritus Professor of Ethology, tells me he used it shortly afterwards 'in a keynote address at a conference in Boston and a lot of people at the conference were rather shocked!'. I doubt if Darwin's core message would have shocked any of us.

## PROFESSOR JENNY CLACK FRS

Jenny Clack is a Curator at the Museum of Zoology and Professor of Vertebrate Palaeontology. She has been a Fellow of Darwin College since 1997. In 2008 she was awarded the Daniel Giraud Eliot Medal by the US National Academy of Sciences for her work on the evolutionary development of early tetrapods. While conducting research as a graduate student at the University of Newcastle, she made a number of discoveries which shed new light on the development of ears in early tetrapods. Following completion of her PhD, she uncovered previously misidentified fossil fragments of a tetrapod called *Acanthostega* in the Department of Earth Sciences at Cambridge. Using the expedition notes from this previous find, she mounted an expedition to Greenland in 1987 and was able to collect and identify several more specimens. These finds, together with subsequent finds of *ichthyostega* and carboniferous *chondrichthyans*, have enabled her to extend current thinking about the transition of vertebrate life from water to land. Her most recent research using x-ray technology and advanced data extraction protocols has shed new light on the structure of vertebrae in tetrapods, and consequently on their mobility, and of their rib cages.

*Professor Jenny Clack on her motorbike.*

## PROGRAMME

Conference sessions are at the University Music School in West Road. Participants are asked to arrive *five minutes before each session* to enable a prompt start.

SUNDAY 27 JUNE

7 p.m.    **Reception and Buffet at Darwin College**

MONDAY 28 JUNE

Morning Session Chairman: Lord Todd
**1  GENERAL INTRODUCTION**
9.45 a.m.    Welcome by Professor Sir Moses Finley, Master of Darwin College
9.55    Dr S. Brenner, Medical Research Council Laboratory of Molecular Biology, Cambridge
11.15    *Coffee*
**2  EVOLUTIONARY HISTORY**
11.45–12.50  INTRODUCTION
Professor E. Mayr, Harvard University
\*\*\*

Afternoon Session Chairman: Professor Sir Moses Finley
2.30 p.m.    THE ORIGINS AND DEVELOPMENT OF DARWIN'S THEORISING
Dr M. J. S. Hodge, University of Leeds
3.20    DARWIN'S PHILOSOPHICAL METHOD
Professor D. L. Hull, University of Wisconsin, Milwaukee
4.10    *Tea*
4.40–5.30    TWENTIETH CENTURY DEVELOPMENTS
Professor G. E. Allen, Washington University, St. Louis

TUESDAY 29 JUNE

Morning Session Chairman: Dr W. F. Bodmer
**3  MOLECULAR AND CELLULAR EVOLUTION**
9 a.m.    MOLECULAR EVOLUTION
Professor L. E. Orgel, the Salk Institute
9.50    MOLECULAR TINKERING OF EVOLUTION
Dr F. Jacob, Institut Pasteur, Paris
10.40    *Coffee*
11.10    PROTEIN DOMAINS
Professor Sir David Phillips, Oxford University
12–12.50  ORIGIN OF SELF-REPLICATING SYSTEMS
Professor Dr M. Eigen, Max Planck Institut für biophysikalische Chemie, Göttingen
\*\*\*

Afternoon Session Chairman: Professor L. E. Orgel
2.30 p.m.    VARIATION AS A GENETIC ENGINEERING PROCESS
Dr J. Shapiro, University of Chicago
3.20    EVOLUTION OF GENE FAMILIES: THE GLOBIN GENES
Dr A. Jeffreys, University of Leicester
4.10    *Tea*
4.40–5.30    GENE CLUSTERING AND GENOME EVOLUTION
Dr W. F. Bodmer, Imperial Cancer Research Fund Laboratories, London
6 p.m.    **Reception at Christ's College**

WEDNESDAY 30 JUNE

Session Chairman: Dr S. Brenner
9 a.m.    MOLECULAR ASPECTS OF EVOLUTION IN BACTERIA
Professor C. R. Woese, University of Illinois

9.50    EXPERIMENTAL EVOLUTION
Professor P. H. Clarke, University College, London
10.40    *Coffee*
11.10–12  MITOCHONDRIAL DNA AND THE EVOLUTION OF HOMINOIDS
Professor A. Wilson, University of California, Berkeley
\*\*\*

*Free afternoon*
6 p.m.    **Vice-Chancellor's Reception in the University Combination Room**
8.30    **Darwin Centenary Concert**

THURSDAY 1 JULY

Session Chairman: Professor J. Maynard Smith
**4  EVOLUTION OF WHOLE ORGANISMS**
9 a.m.    ORGANISM AND ENVIRONMENT, THE PARADOX OF ADAPTATION
Professor R. C. Lewontin, Harvard University
9.50    POPULATION GENETICS AND ECOLOGY – THE INTERFACE
Professor E. Nevo, University of Haifa
10.40    *Coffee*
11.10    EVOLUTION AND ECOLOGY IN PLANTS
Professor J. C. Harper, University College of North Wales
12–12.50  PALAEONTOLOGY AND MACROEVOLUTIONARY THEORY
Professor S. J. Gould, Harvard University
\*\*\*

2.30 p.m.    PLATE TECTONICS AND EVOLUTION
Professor A. Hallam, University of Birmingham
3.20    UNIVERSAL DARWINISM
Dr R. Dawkins, Oxford University
4.10    *Tea*
4.40–5.30    MICROEVOLUTION AND MACROEVOLUTION
Professor F. J. Ayala, University of California, Davis
8.30    David Attenborough will introduce sequences from a new BBC series of ecological films. *Lady Mitchell Hall, Sidgwick Avenue.*

FRIDAY 2 JULY

Morning Session Chairman: Dr B. A. O. Williams
**5  EVOLUTION OF SOCIAL BEHAVIOUR**
9 a.m.    DEVELOPMENT OF AN EVOLUTIONARY ETHOLOGY
Professor R. W. Burkhardt, University of Illinois, Urbana
9.50    EVOLUTIONARY STRATEGIES
Professor J. Maynard Smith, University of Sussex
10.40    *Coffee*
11.10    REPRODUCTIVE SUCCESS AND THE EVOLUTION OF REPRODUCTIVE STRATEGIES IN MALES AND FEMALES
Dr T. H. Clutton-Brock, King's College, Cambridge
12–12.50  RULES FOR CHANGING THE RULES
Dr P. P. G. Bateson, Cambridge University
\*\*\*

Afternoon Session Chairman: Professor J. Passmore
2.30 p.m.    HUMAN EVOLUTION
Professor G. Isaac, University of California, Berkeley
3.20    SOCIOBIOLOGY
Professor E. O. Wilson, Harvard University
4.10    *Tea*
4.40    EVOLUTION AND ETHICS
Dr B. A. O. Williams, King's College, Cambridge
5.30    Closing address by Professor J. Passmore, Australian National University
7.30    **Conference Dinner at Queen's College**

**Evolution of Molecules and Men**

**DARWIN CENTENARY CONFERENCE**
27 June – 2 July 1982
**Darwin College, Cambridge, England**

*Programme and cover for the Darwin Centenary Conference Programme.*

# POETS CORNER

## GEORGE GÖMÖRI
**Mari Gömöri**

Darwin College has been home to many internationally renowned scientists, but perhaps not quite as many famous literary figures.

An exception to this is Emeritus Fellow George Gömöri, whom the older members of the College will know mainly for his many years of teaching Polish and Hungarian literature, and for his political activities during the 1956 Hungarian Revolution. George has edited *The Darwinian* for several years together with Andrew Prentice and served on the Meals Committee, fighting to improve standards.

What they may not know is that George is an award-winning poet, having published 12 books of poetry in Hungarian, and four co-translated with Clive Wilmer in English. Here below are a couple from his time in Cambridge. Coincidentally George's home with his first wife, 55 Eltisley Avenue, had also been the house where Ted Hughes and Sylvia Plath lived during their time together in Cambridge. His home with his present wife Mari was 46 Grantchester Road, see below.

### At Times Like This
*towards the end of October*
*when the huge chestnut spreading its branches*

*majestically at the gates of King's College*
*turns to the colour of clear honey*
*and the medlar decks itself out in shades of copper*
*and the small fig bares its branches*
*no longer concealing the slightness of its yield*
*at times like this at the turn of autumn*
*I hear once again the bugle-call*
*sounding from faraway*
*just moments before the parade*
*and the most abandoned carnival\* in our history*
*began*

[translated by Clive Wilmer and George Gömöri]
*\*allusion to the student march, which escalated into the Hungarian Revolution of 1956*

### 46 Grantchester Road
*With you twenty-four years*
*in the same house in good cheer,*
*in joy, sorrow, alarm,*
*in a wild thunderstorm;*
*with a child, then with children,*
*With what you planted there*

**Opposite:** *György Gömöri by Jenő Medveczky.*

George has also been the subject of many television programmes in Hungary and has sat for some of the leading Hungarian artists, sculptors and photographers.

The painting of the 24-year-old George – that is György Gömöri – is by his late stepfather, Jenő Medveczky, one of the leading Hungarian painters of the 20th century, the bronze bust is by Imre Varga, whose oeuvre includes sculptures in the Vatican museum, as well as a full-length statue of Béla Bartok in Kensington, London. George and his wife Mari have also been photographed by the Hungarian photographer Otto Kaiser, who recently had an exhibition in London.

## ONE LONG, GOLDEN SUMMER
### Kathy Wheeler

The Darwin College of the mid 1970s was a joy for many of us first-year PhD students coming from abroad. For a foreign student, the ease of making acquaintances and even friends banished the inevitable dreary loneliness within a week of our arrival.

One rare, long summer – when I had a glorious room on the ground floor of the Rayne Building overlooking the pastures and the River Cam – the weather was extraordinarily memorable, and made for some wonderful experiences. All of June, July, August, even September of 1976 was a king's feast of sun and warmth, day after yellow, sun-drenched day. Every morning that bright and shining summer of 1976, I would take a coffee and sit outside about 6.30, to watch the cows strolling back towards College to graze on the grassy-green meadows, their soft lowing mixed with early-morning bird songs. The moisture rising from the river and the emerald-green fields nearby veiled the brown and white cows in mistiness, giving them a dream-like, supernatural quality. But the reality of an empty stomach lured one away for breakfast, even from the peace and softness of the rural scene.

*in the well-mown back garden –*
*a large lilac tree.*
*With windows looking out*
*on a field that is always green,*
*with books on the upstairs landing*
*shelved all along the wall,*
*with downstairs a crippled piano,*
*a statuette and pictures*
*in the spacious room at the back.*
*With the hollyhock I wrote*
*a poem about in front,*
*and if there was trouble between us,*
*you bore it as I bore it.*
*Twenty-four years it has been*
*in the house we leave today;*
*twenty-four years, twenty-four;*
*let's start counting anew.*

[Translated by Clive Wilmer and George Gömöri]

Wanting the afternoons of that matchless summer to be wholly free for outdoor enjoyments, I would turn to the desk with determination and, from 7am to 2pm, write up my doctorate, chapter after gruelling chapter – all those four months long – sustained by occasional musings on the picturesque scene outside, framed perfectly by a huge window. The bright promise of afternoon delights made the hours fly, for after work, we would go punting up the Cam to Grantchester, with not infrequent (but unintentional) dunkings in the river, as the punt pole got stuck in its muddy bottom, and left one hanging for a few breathtaking, airy seconds as the punt sailed on. Or we took long walks north, down the river towards Ely Cathedral, whose spires cut through the deep-blue sky and floated mirage-like on the gleaming fens ahead. We made a rare trip out in the fens to Geoffrey Keynes' country house to be ravished by his incomparable collection of William Blake's gold-illuminated manuscripts, and where he made us welcome, and had his housekeeper serve tea and almond-paste cakes. Or we raced across the Grantchester field paths to Byron's Pool, and cooled off in the chilly brown waters. Sometimes we cycled to Trumpington village church and collapsed among mossy, grey-green headstones, mouldy

in the warm dampness. And there were dashing bike rides to the eastern Gog Magog Hills. For the Hills, we always took hampers full of mouth-watering orange, red, green, yellow, and rich brown delicacies: smoked salmon sandwiches, cherry tomatoes with bunches of watercress, fresh, real chicken liver paté, stilton from the market cheese man, red-gold apricots and deep-purple grapes, and big chunks of dark brown bread from the Newnham bakery. After breaking out this feast about 3pm, for a late, hard-earned lunch (those long working mornings!), we would loll in the shade of giant elms, or stroll through Miltonic 'cool colonnades', before mounting our bikes for the wild, downhill race homeward, at breakneck speed, along Hills Road into town.

Once back at College, more than likely our Italian opera bass Mario (a student of Charles Darwin's papers) would be strolling through the Rayne Building in the early evenings, making the corridors ring with his deep-voiced snippets of Puccini and Verdi, Rossini, Bellini and Donizetti. That in itself was an education, not only in opera but in singing, as he painstakingly but genially explained the ins and out of operatic techniques. And so we piled into Hall for supper, dining as much on each other's enthusiasm for genetics or Coleridge, black holes or European history, or the beauty of partial differential equations. If luck that evening decided to be truly profligate, we might, at coffee in the Parlour, be enchanted by the law student from New Mexico, with marvellous stories of her dealings, as Assistant Attorney General, with Navajo, Pueblo, Zuni and other tribes' affairs.

That rare and blissful summer, with its innumerable moments of turquoise enchantments inlaid into the hard but shining silver of our working days, was itself a work of art, enriching a past that still illuminates the present, its light and colours unfading after three decades. There was never another to match it.

*Daphne Angus, Dean's secretary 1974–84.*

## RESEARCHING BLUNDEN'S SECRETS
### Sumie Okada

It was raining when I first arrived at Darwin College as a visiting scholar in the late 1970s. Before then I had been at Lady Margaret Hall, Oxford, as a recipient of a Fellowship from my university in Tokyo. The gate of Lady Margaret Hall was like the entrance to a medieval castle. In comparison with that, Darwin looked like a very small college to me, with only glass doors. To be honest, when I first arrived there I was a bit worried whether this was a good college or not. As it turned out, I soon realised how silly I was!

The room I was allocated was on the top floor of the Rayne Building, whose rooms were reserved for mature women, visiting scholars or PhD students. There were several visiting scholars from Japan at Darwin then and the Dean's secretary, Daphne Angus, looked after us all very well.

*The bust of Charles Darwin on the stairs in Newnham Grange.*

Entering the flat through the wooden front door, there was a small shower room on the right, and on the left was a wardrobe. The main room was in Scandinavian style with wooden walls designed to retain the heat, and just one large window looking down the narrow stream of the River Cam, where occasional punting made the atmosphere livelier, and I very much enjoyed the running streams below my window. Darwin College has such a good location, near to the University Library and Sidgwick site where all the lectures organised by the English faculty were held. The University Centre across the river had large windows in the coffee lounge which overlooked the back of Darwin College. I had the pleasure of dining there with my friends, enjoying the view. Of course I also dined at Darwin, where very impressive black tables welcomed all the graduate members. I often dined there and very seldom had to resort to my own rather poor Japanese cooking. The Darwin dining room was open to the meadows and the River Cam and was full of light.

One of the most memorable and significant events which happened to me at that time was that I met Mrs Claire Blunden, the third wife of Edmund Blunden, the World War I poet and friend of Siegfried Sassoon. I met her through the introduction of my Japanese professor.

She kindly invited me to her home in Mawson Road, mentioning that there were many letters sent to Aki Hayashi, Blunden's Japanese friend and asking me if I would be interested in sorting them out. It turned out that Aki was not only a friend and secretary, but also his lover. Her existence was very little known to Blunden's English and Japanese friends. In 1928 Blunden was Professor of English at the prestigious Tokyo University. They first met in the famous summer resort, Karuizawa, when Aki Hayashi, an English teacher, was a participant in the summer school where he was a lecturer. They began a relationship and Blunden, although married to his first wife in England with two children, brought Aki to England. She died in a lonely bedsit in Hampstead, London, keeping Blunden's letters, chronicling their 36-year relationship in detail, carefully and neatly under her bed.

Claire Blunden brought all the letters very casually on her bicycle to my room in Darwin, and soon I had a great task of taking copies of the 1,400 letters, because all the original versions had to be returned to her. I used Darwin's copying room and completed the task with the help and company of my friend, Yasuko Shimizu, another Japanese visiting scholar. I still remember that the copying machine was a bit high for me so I had to use a stool. The Darwin Porters kindly let me do the copying without asking anything.

In 1981 I transferred to Emmanuel College to do my MLitt thesis, which was published in 1988 by MacMillan and entitled *Edmund Blunden and Japan: the history of a relationship*. Professor John Bayley from Oxford, who was my tutor at that time, wrote my introduction, and his famous novelist wife, Iris Murdoch, also wrote a short recommendation. It was also translated into Japanese. However, the most significant research I did at Cambridge was in those copies made at Darwin.

*Opposite: May Ball, 2012.*

## WORDSWORTH'S RHYTHMS
### Walter Bernhardt

When I arrived at Cambridge in the autumn of 1973 and joined Darwin as what was then called a category III member I did so with a sense of achievement. I had recently been awarded my doctorate by the University of Graz for a metrical study of Wordsworth's *Prelude*, which used the then latest and most-advanced methods of linguistic and structuralist analysis. Yet at Cambridge I had to start all over again. The English Department was puzzling to my theory-infected mind, but stimulation and encouragement came from the College: when sitting next to a biologist at lunch and between an endocrinologist and an ethologist at dinner (with Jaros the Butler serving wine more generously than usual) the mind inevitably opened up. The fruits were seen in my further work in the field of rhythmic studies, and I am ever grateful to Graham Hough, my unobtrusive mentor on untrodden ways in the realms of English Literature, for being such a wonderful guide and inspirer. Coming from Austria, I found the College's multi-national climate congenial, and I also found there expressions of that sense of conflicting ambivalence which – for better or worse – characterises many attitudes in my own home country. I returned several times to benefit from the boon of scholarly inspiration and was always made welcome. With its climate of gentle encouragement, the College has been a constant haven of quiet and repose to the nomadic scholar, for whom Cambridge still preserves some of the old monastic qualities of its early origins.

# DARWIN COLLEGE STUDENTS ASSOCIATION

Darwin College Students Association is the body which brings together the social and sporting activities of the College in one committee. Its first order of business at its inaugural meeting on 17 November 1965 was the election of a committee, closely followed by a discussion of the amenities the association wished to provide for the then tiny student body. Top of the list was a punt.

Clearly, a college with such a close relationship with the river required boats, but Chester White, who became the first DCSA Treasurer, was the only rower, so a formal boat club was not then possible. A punt was duly bought for £50 in spring 1966. In fact, the first sports club to be discussed by the DCSA was a cricket club, which Julian Paren wished to found in April 1967, and the first Darwin sporting facility besides the punt was a

*Left: DCSA committee, 2012–13.*

**Opposite:** *May Ball, 2013.*

## CHERRY MUIJSSON, DCSA PRESIDENT 2012–13

Being President of the Darwin College Students Association for the 2012–13 academic year was especially exciting, with the inauguration of a new Master, Professor Mary Fowler, as well as the historic opportunity to meet His Royal Highness the Duke of Cambridge during his first visit to Cambridge since he was granted his title.

Student life and participation was at an all-time high in Darwin, with the College claiming the mantle of having organised the most Freshers' week events of any Cambridge college in 2012. Furthermore, we also hosted several spectacularly successful events including Chinese New Year, Burns Night and our annual Sports Day, where Darwin competed with determination against our Oxford sister college, Wolfson. The committee also dedicated funding towards a new ladies' rowing boat, a renovation of the TV room and the extension of the societies roll list.

The Darwin community has really proved itself to be both the centre and the envy of the graduate community in Cambridge.

croquet set bought that summer. A table tennis table was bought for the common room the following year but there were no College facilities for the serious sportsperson. Students were obliged to join the clubs of other colleges and, initially, paid their own subscriptions. In 1969, however, Patrick Sherry, then DCSA Chair, negotiated an agreement with Gonville and Caius whereby the DCSA would pay a subscription allowing any Darwin student to join their clubs. Gradually, over the years, the College has negotiated agreements for shared facilities with various colleges as its own clubs have sprung up. There is now a huge array of home-grown sports clubs from the Boat Club to the Basketball Club, including the very successful mixed Cricket Club, Football Clubs, racket sports, swimming and punting, and there is a DCSA Sports Officer to coordinate it all.

The second amenity discussed at that first meeting was the possibility of a May Ball. It was agreed that some form of summer dance would take place, perhaps in two years. In the event, a summer dance was indeed held for the first time in 1967 and made a loss of about £10. The tipping point came in the early 1970s, and the May Ball is now the biggest event of the DCSA year, and never makes a loss. Other firsts in 1967 included the purchase of a piano and the production of a play, *The Flies* by Sartre, directed by Susan Aaronson. Darwin drama flourished under the stewardship of Hugh

Mellor in the 1980s and 1990s but relies on the enthusiasm of each new generation of students.

The third item on the inaugural agenda was the acquisition of a Pye television set for the common room and, right at the bottom of the list, a barrel of beer. This was the modest beginning of what has become one of Cambridge's most successful student bars, after formal organisation of a bar service took place in 1968. The bar now occupies much of the road frontage of the Hermitage and its walls are testament to the Darwinian passion for sports.

CW

## COLLEGE BOATS

Now more than 40 years old, the Darwin College Boat Club (DCBC) can trace its origins to the enthusiasm of its founder, sometime Senior Treasurer and *éminence grise*, Chester White. Dr Chester White came to Cambridge in 1961 as House Surgeon in the new neurosciences unit at Addenbrooke's Hospital. After moving briefly into gynaecology, he applied for research in haematology under Frank Hayhoe, who was one of the founding Fellows of Darwin College and its first Vice-Master. Thus Chester

*Opposite: Oars in the Darwin bar.*

*Above: Chester White, founder of DCBC, with Torsten Krude, 2012.*

*Right: Lent Bumps, 2013.*

*Opposite inset: First year's accounts for DCBC, showing the purchase of the* Hugo de Balsham *from Peterhouse.*

White became one of the earliest students at Darwin in 1965. He was also the only rower in the student body and was able to introduce his colleagues to the pleasures of boating by discovering and restoring an old Darwin family skiff in the Old Granary, with the help of the Bursar, Bill Stuart-Clark. A punt was then bought, while Chester maintained his interest in rowing by coaching boats at Peterhouse, the sister college to his Oxford alma mater, Merton, and subsequently rowing with medical colleagues at Clare College. This connection led to Clare lending Darwin its first IV in 1967. Gradually, interest in rowing increased, until by 1970 there were about 20 rowers in College, the women using CUWBC and the men joining Peterhouse Boat Club as individuals. Fortunately for Darwin, Peterhouse Boat Club underwent a lean period at about this

time, and Chester was able to persuade them to sell Darwin both an old clinker VIII, named the *Hugo de Balsham,* and its oars, for £145 in February 1971, just in time for the Lents. However, a dispute soon arose with the Bumps Committee of CUBC when the proposed first-ever Darwin boat crew included women, reflecting Darwin's status as Cambridge's first co-educational college. A couple of replacement men were hastily pressed into the crew but another hurdle presented itself: it was necessary to qualify with a time trial. Sadly, with so little preparation, and blades hastily

ACCOUNTS 1970-71     DARWIN COLLEGE
CAMBRIDGE
CB3 9EU
0223-6780-3

SUBSCRIPTIONS PAID DIRECTLY TO PETERHOUSE

| | DEBITS | CREDITS |
|---|---|---|
| Loan from College (Repayable by DCSA) | — | £150.00 |
| PURCHASE of BOAT | £60.00 | — |
| " OARS | £85.00 | — |
| May Races Entry fee | £4.00 | — |
| C.U B.C. Rule Book | £0.25 | — |
| Registration with Cam. Row. Assoc (Town Bumps) | £1.50 | — |
| July Races Entry fee | £1.25 | — |
| July Subscriptions | £12.00 | £12.00 |
| Churchill B.C. fee | £10.00 | |
| | £162.00 | £162.00 |

changed to Darwin's colours with the aid of insulating tape as there was no time to repaint them, the fledgling crew failed to qualify. Returning to the fray in the Mays 1971, a resurgent VIII determined to do better, duly qualified, but, misunderstanding the time between the starting guns, were caught unprepared, with their oars on the bank, and got off to a disastrous start, hauling themselves from tussock to grassy tussock. The nascent Boat Club received its first official funding from the DCSA in December 1971, with which it was able to negotiate to share Peterhouse's boathouse and facilities. Within a very short time, despite this inglorious debut, Darwin had produced its first rowing Blue in Helen McFie, and the Boat Club has been one of the most consistently popular clubs at Darwin ever since.

Darwin's most distinguished rower to date has been Nonie Ray, who competed in the Women's Double Sculls at the 1984 Los Angeles Olympics while working on her PhD in Earth Sciences (she was allowed to intermit two terms).

**CW** and **ELG**

*The first Darwin Ladies crews.* **Above:** *Mays 1979. L–R Carol Williams, Jane Lawry, Sue Bayliss, Tessa McRae and, cox, C.J. Freeman.*
**Below:** *1970. Cox: Mary Evans, with Jill Parsons, Prudence Nicol, Mavis Fewtrell, Jenny Lord, Helen McFie, Gudrun Politt, Valery Myers and Carol Williams.*

## Golden Years

### Tamas Bertenyi

The middle of the 1990s represented a renaissance of the Darwin College Boat Club. If one had to put a specific date on it, perhaps it would be 1995. This was when Torsten Krude (then a young-ish Junior Research Fellow in College) took on the unglamorous role of captain in a small graduate college boat club that was not on anyone's Cambridge rowing radar. He brought together a loyal, if somewhat quixotic, cadre of rowers assisted by experienced coaching from out of College. DCBC was able to buy a new (to them) boat and eventually even 'modern' cleavers. But change takes time, and the inertia of a languid club is not quick to turn around. The members of DCBC knew then (as it remains true to this day) that the success of a club is not as much dependent on that day's rowing victories but the continuity and long-term stability of the institution. To that end, senior members were required to recruit and coach the next years' cohorts, and a proactive effort was maintained to keep the club healthy and happy. Just as important as training was to nurture the camaraderie and deep bonds that the Boat Club's social dimension brought to the game.

Within a season or two, the reinvigorated Boat Club started to show serious results. It can be argued that having a graduate college of full-grown men and women was a definite boon. Many a Darwin 1st VIII were known to casually walk up and down the tow path before the one-minute gun went off at the bumps, nonchalantly impressing this fact upon the scrawny half-grown pimply-faced bed-wetting undergrads in adjacent boats. But that isn't to take away from the sheer determination and enthusiasm of the individuals and the club as a whole. In the year of Torsten's captaincy, the 1st Men won blades in the Lents and the Mays for the first time in years. By the

time of Karin Tybjerg and Paul Johnson's captainships in 1997, the mighty Darwin Machine was carving up the river at full steam. That year alone, four Darwin boats won blades in the Mays. The exception was the Men's 2nd VIII, which didn't just go up four, but actually managed a double over-bump. This was a feat of nautical domination not topped for a decade and half, until the 2012 Darwin Fellows Boat achieved a triple over-bump. That Fellows Boat's captain? A now slightly grey but just as enthusiastic Torsten Krude. The 1997 Women's 1st VIII (by this time confidently referred to as the Darwinator Crew) went up a stunning nine places with three normal bumps and two over-bumps to make it into the second division for the first time. During these years, both the women's and men's crews were finishing at the top of the Fairbairns races, with the women coming in second in 2000.

Rowing was a different world in those days, and corporate sponsorship of college crews, especially graduate colleges in lower divisions, was unheard of. The Boat Club subsisted on generous support from College and a few rather heroic fundraising campaigns by its members. This ranged from structured activities, such as the epic 24-hour sponsored 'erg' of 1998, to more ad hoc events, such as one initiated by Kirk Salveson, who – having for the entirety of that year sported a bushy blonde moustache and hairdo best described as '1970s Scandinavian Porn Star Chic' – passed the old whip-around in the bar, agreeing to have his trademark hirsuteness shaved off if sufficient funds were raised for the Boat Club. Targets were exceeded, resulting in even his head being shaved clean. Apparently, his own mother failed to recognise him.

Possibly the most impressive statistic was that in 1999, with the club captains Erik Lithander and Ruth Hamilton, there was a total of seven Darwin crews in the Mays. Considering Darwin College only had a few hundred students at this time, this marked a phenomenal engagement by the student body. During these years, Darwin was often a contender for the Michell Cup of best-performing boat club. Season after season, Darwin crews raked in rowing triumphs and an almost embarrassing

*The Mays 2000 'Ladies' 3rd Boat.*

number of blades. To this day, the Darwin bar plays host to some of these trophy blades and a decade's worth of Boat Club portraits.

The long-term success of the Boat Club and its sheer volume of current and recent rowers (back when the majority of College members were PhD students and tended to hang around for three or four or sometimes five years) allowed for the assembling of some formidable Darwin journeyman Bumps crews. The 'Darwin Gents' crew of Mays 2000, which featured four different personnel configurations on four different days, and whose only training as a team was to row to the start line, famously achieved a bump in 19 strokes on its way to winning blades. They also introduced a new gold standard in alcohol bans for bumps preparation: 'Once you've pushed off on your way to the start, no more opening new drinks. If you have one open already, however, you are of course allowed to finish it.' For many years, the fine tradition of Darwin Ladies' and Gentlemen's crews, stocked with experienced but now half-retired first boaters, wreaked havoc in the lower divisions.

It was also at this time that a unique chapter in DCBC's history was written. Chester White happened to be in touch with one Artur da Silva Pinto. Artur was Portuguese, and with the support of EU funding he was

determined to introduce Portugal to Oxbridge and vice versa. In the summer of 1998, therefore, a contingent of Darwin rowers and choir members, together with their Oxford counterparts from Wolfson, descended upon Porto and the Douro river valley, hosted by the Associaçao de Antigos Alunos da Universidade do Porto.

A portion of the time was spent upriver in the ancient city of Lamego. A large dam on the river made for the most impressive training stretch, unimaginable to those brought up in their rowing careers on the twisty, grown-in and often dark and freezing River Cam, overcrowded with novice crews pointed in every direction at once. At the end of the week, a pair of traditional skiffs took the entire contingent – two colleges' worth of women and men rowers, coxes, groupies and coaches as well as the choir – back to Porto, where the final regatta was to be held. This race took place on the widest part of the river (under questionable hygienic conditions) between the old bridges, and marked by massive waves which threatened to stop the boats in their tracks as the boats' riggers crashed into their

tops. Nonetheless, Darwin emerged triumphant in both the men's and women's races. The two biggest years for these Porto trips were 1999 and 2000, and the choir was fortunate enough to follow up with another visit in 2002. To this day, many a DCBC alumnus holds a strong affection for the beautiful city of Porto and the Douro river valley.

Ultimately, the pinnacle of this era for DCBC has to be the beginning of the 2000s. It can be taken as a proud testament by all members of the Boat Club that during this period Darwin produced a succession of women University rowers. Starting with Beth Davidson, no fewer than 11 DCBC women represented the University at the Oxford–Cambridge Boat Races: Sarah Molton, Ellen Nisbet, Ella Palmer, Anna Reinicke, Caroline Cowan, Vanessa Murrie, Renae Domaschenz, Tamsin Eades, Holly Rogers and (a few years later) Evgenia Ilyinskaya either rowed in the heavyweight and lightweight CUWBC crews or were coxes. Not surprisingly, at the same time the Women's 1st VIII achieved the highest position of any Darwin boat in the 2004 May Bumps, when they made it into the first division.

*Rowing on the massive Douro River on a hot Portuguese summer day seemed a million miles away from the cold, dark, rainy winter mornings on the Cam.*

*The Portugal trips weren't just about rowing and singing; we were there to live and breathe the culture that Porto and the north of Portugal had to offer. This ranged from touring quintas to visiting historical sites to drinking beers long into the hot summer nights in the Darwin-designated Superbock Square of old Porto.*

## INTERNATIONAL HARMONY: CROSSING BORDERS WITH THE DARWIN CHOIR
### Alan Blackwell

It's a long way from Andean llama songs, Czech opera and shape note singing of the Southern USA to English folk music on a pleasure cruise along the Douro River in Portugal. But this was the trajectory of a little Iberian Renaissance – a small but significant high point of Darwin cultural life.

Research Fellow Henry Stobart, the ethnomusicologist and llama afficionado, injected a huge dose of musical enthusiasm to the College, notably in the lecture series 'Sound' (1997), which in addition to the standard Friday lectures, promised a concert or sound event every week in Lent. That sonic momentum continued in an informal choir conducted by regular summer visitor Alan Swanson (an American teaching Swedish at the University of Groningen), who recognised that the limited musical range of Darwin students could be addressed with 'Old Possum's Guide to Reading Music' – his two-page introduction to everything needed for basic choral competence. Finally, the uncommon arrival of a Darwin PhD student in music brought us the great asset of Dimitra Stamogiannou, who sacrificed days and weeks of her PhD (on Czech composer Janáček) to learn the skills and repertoire of a choir conductor.

These preparations allowed us to seize the opportunity to join the boat clubs of Darwin and our Oxford sister Wolfson in a trip to Porto. Just as the tradition of the Oxford–Cambridge Boat Race is celebrated in Portugal, so is the tradition of choral music from the two Universities. Hearing that Darwin College had acquired a choir, it was proposed that the two colleges should also undertake a choral tour, alongside a series of races between the College boat clubs in 1999.

The practical gulf from 'Old Possum's Guide' to an international concert tour will be glaringly apparent. The core half-dozen singers from Alan and Dimitra's choirs were expanded to 20, with the additional challenge that several of that core were also rowers, so had to choose

## STEFAN PAETKE

My experiences of Darwin were thoroughly different to those of my previous three years spent at Cambridge. In the late 1970s most colleges found postgraduates a strange and exotic species to be at best tolerated, but not really welcomed. I knew I needed somewhere very different, and was introduced to Darwin by Jenny and David Edmonds (my supervisor). Darwin in 1975 already attracted an astonishing variety of people, most of whom had not previously studied in Cambridge and many not from the UK, and this decisively contributed to its remarkable depth and vibrancy. Postgraduates were encouraged to be involved with the College to the extent they wished: some regarded Darwin as merely a University 'requirement', others as a place to have lunch and show family and friends the Cambridge 'experience', but many became wholeheartedly involved in the life of the College.

I was fortunate to live in a large room in the Old Granary overlooking the river for over two years, possibly down to my tenures as DCSA Chairman and Boat Club Captain in successive years. This prime location encouraged, and sometimes required involvement in College activities but also allowed the easy enjoyment of the delightful College gardens (and not just stumbling home from the enticing College bar, to be clear!). Mind you, the bay window did blow a gale in the winter (until I reattached it to the frame), you really could cook an egg on top of the storage heater and I never did manage to silence the duck 'dawn chorus'. However, the fire hoist proved dramatically successful one night when tested by a volunteer resident to appreciative crowds outside. Of course, order of a sort was normally maintained by the remarkable Mrs P.

However, for me the start of regular and well-attended seminars on a wide variety of subjects from our postgraduates and Fellows (later followed by the Darwin College Lecture Series) were a mark that Darwin was beginning to come of age.

There were many postgraduate and senior members who inspired, and often challenged, me in my time at Darwin; I will mention three. The inimitable Mike Crosthwait, who could be relied on to be at the start of a cold Bumps race and usually to push the boat out in their ultimate allegiance to sport or culture. In a second year, the traditional Darwin welcome to guests from town or gown was an essential asset, with several enthusiastic choristers recruited from nearby offices. The author persuaded his wife to join the choir as soprano soloist, and contacts with Girton identified a small group of undergraduate chapel singers who selflessly accepted an expenses-paid summer holiday in Portugal.

Having acted as tour manager, I find many adventures and emergencies recorded in a file of over 2,000 email messages. There was a great deal of assistance from Research Fellow, rehearsal accompanist and Music Committee Secretary Elisabeth Hill, who didn't even get a trip to Portugal. Having recruited local music teacher Mark Mason as touring conductor, a rapid progression of his recently diagnosed multiple sclerosis left us looking for a replacement the week before the tour (Oxford conductor Jennifer Bailey stepped in, learned the Cambridge repertoire, and conducted both choirs). But the most vivid of my memories is negotiating entry to the venue for our first concert in Porto, only to discover that the cathedral organ was being dismantled by a man with an angle-grinder, who had just finished stacking its pipes at the side of the nave. Our request for an organ initiated an exciting day of technical discussions (largely in Portuguese) about synthesisers and powerful amps, eventually borrowed from the rock band friends of a Portuguese choir member.

The overall standard, however, was so high that we were immediately invited to return for a second tour the following year. In 2000, we acquired our own conductor,

*A Darwin duck.*

a good direction, and who really could not understand why stamping the full address on College house keys was a security issue, and felt constrained to argue to severely limit spending on refurbishing some really appalling College accommodation. 'Rum and Black' Jack (Hicks), who looked after us all and gave me an already venerable Christmas cactus, which continues in rude health. Particularly I cherish the wisdom, humour and generosity that I found in Moses Finley. This was

a period of change and development at the College, and we would discuss many issues at length and with delightful candour, as I stayed upwind to reduce my smoke inhalation. His tenure as Master involved much change, for some painful, and a genuine recognition of the seriousness of a number of issues, particularly accommodation shortages, as well as many management, academic and social developments.

Darwin has given me good friends, a 'home' for occasional visits and happy memories. The Boat Club introduced me to both the joys and pains of rowing (I still manage to avoid lower back surgery … or is this just the result of old age?). There are memories of fine rowers, and our delightful and ruthlessly effective cox Rachel Barker, who usually did not chain smoke in the boat, and only left the boat once when it was in midstream, to be rescued by gallant crew members and bank party. I still have fine addictions to wine (I would like that to be fine wine) and the London Silver Vaults (the latter after visiting with Gordon Robin to buy Frank Young's leaving gift).

Matthew Steynor, a talented young organ scholar whom we head-hunted from Queens' College, luring him across Silver Street with the promise of Portuguese sun. We assembled a programme showcasing the English choral repertoire – Parry, Skempton, Weelkes and Vaughan Williams – as well as a nod to the culture of our hosts with the *Crux Fidelis* attributed to John IV of Portugal.

These two tours were remarkable milestones in the history of Darwin College. Although there are many colleges in Cambridge that one might turn to as exemplars of the choral music tradition, Darwin's strengths have generally been in other areas. Darwinians arriving with a prior interest in singing generally seek opportunities at a college where there is a chapel, an organ and established posts for organ scholars and directors of music.

Nevertheless, these tours resulted in several generations of Darwinians who take pride in a short but respectable career as international performing artists.

## PUNTS
### Donald Nicolson
The College has an enormous river frontage so punts were a feature from its first days and even earlier. In the 1890s, well before Newnham Grange became home to the College, George Darwin's daughters Gwen and Margaret spent much of their childhood 'messing about in boats' in their primitive garden punt, as Margaret describes in her memoir.

When I arrived 30 years ago, the College's five punts were managed in a very simple way, as the numbers were so much smaller and life more easy-going. The keys were kept in an open basket on a table in the Old Granary but this led to abuses, when people snaffled them to be sure of a trip the next day. Later they were in a locked cabinet in the Parlour with weekly booking sheets, which I used to print out so that members could claim a slot. After further disputes, the Porters took over the booking and issuing of the keys, and thanks to them the job has been done efficiently ever since.

Punting has been a large part of my life since I came to Darwin. On arrival I joined the Punting Society and soon picked up the idea. Through the years I have done my best for the club in various ways, such as sanding and varnishing the poles and painting College colours on new ones, oiling locks, doing minor repairs, replacing mooring ropes, etc. I was never Admiral; that is – or should be – an arduous task which I would not touch with a punt pole, even though it carries the perk of a room in the Old Granary.

However, my most important gift to the College punters was my short paper entitled 'Basic Punting for Darwinians'. Intended for our frighteningly intelligent would-be doctors and masters, it covers the first principles: 'A punt has two motions, forwards (or backwards) of its central point, and rotary about its centre. Both are achieved with the pole, by bracing the body against it; it is the feet which actually propel and turn the punt, so take a firm stance and maintain it.' And so on.

I bought my first punt, *Daphne* – named after the wonderfully efficient and helpful Dean's secretary, Daphne Angus – from the College when she was damaged and frail with age (the punt, that is). I patched her up and relicensed her as *Victoria R* (after my house and street). The Bursar granted me a mooring at the far end of the garden, where my name is still painted on the wall. The

only access was by the rope ladder I made. He also let me park her for the winter on the Big island where I could re-tar her bottom. She had two successors.

Darwin allowed me to try my hand at many things besides. These included, soon after my arrival, becoming Treasurer of the May Ball, and next year DCSA Treasurer; at various times Chess Club Secretary and Captain, designer of five successive covers (1987/8) for *River Rat*, with each time one more rodent on and around the first bridge – the last daringly descending by parachute; bar servant; compere at Burns Night dinners, etc. I acted in plays, constructed scenery, and controlled the lights for performances. On the Library Committee I rebound books, still to be seen on the shelves, having studied the craft at CCAT, and showed examples of my work

JOIN THE DARWIN ARMADA

DISCOUNTED COCKTAIL EVENT IN DARBAR

EARLY MEMBERSHIP AVAILABLE
FIRST 20 ONLY £25
CASH ONLY

at the lunchtime talk I gave in November 1992. I am so grateful to Darwin for all the opportunities it has given me.

### The Sunken Punt
**Patrick Boner, Gustavo de Britta Rocha, Gordon Euchler and W. Carter Johnson**

While most of us can recall falling out of a punt, few can say they ever sank in one. A small group of Darwinians did just that on an eventful summer evening in 2004.

It began as an end-of-term barbecue on the island, where some alcohol had been consumed. Darwinians of every age were there, including a more senior member, who called for a friendly punt race as the day turned to evening. Our two crowded punts set their course for King's College Chapel, where our race was suddenly cut short by two marauding College members in a kayak. These aspiring pirates have since claimed they were 'simply retaliating against someone's aggression', although the nature and source of this aggression remains uncertain.

The series of events that led to the debacle that day are similarly mysterious. A pole was stolen from a punter, several nervous passengers jumped from one punt to another, and there was a lot of splashing and screaming. As one witness recalls, 'I remember thinking, "Jebus [sic], they're going to sink that punt!" And then, boom! It was underwater.' The sunken punt remained just below the surface, which allowed for a safe return to College. The scene was serene. 'Standing on the stern of a punt exactly three inches underwater,' one witness reports, 'the punter was now impersonating Jebus [sic]'. Once at College, an epic bailing effort put the punt back above water. Were it not that most of the cameras on the expedition – along with several phones and a few sets of keys – were now on the bottom of the Cam, it would have made for a fantastic photograph.

*Inset: The Punting Society poster, 2012.*

*Left: The punts.*

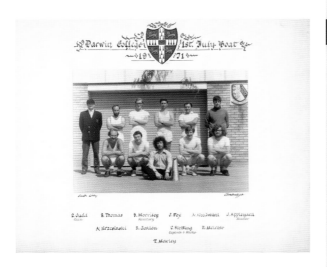

## SPORTS IN THE EARLY YEARS
### Brian Christie

I am told that our year, 1971–2, was the first that produced any full sporting Blues for Darwin, half-Blues having been won by Michael Sik for water polo and Richard Randall for ice hockey in 1968–9. I was the fifth generation of Christie to attend Cambridge and all my ancestors had rowed, so I put myself up for trials for the Blue boat, but without success, and instead somehow found myself coaching Caius' first boat in between rowing with our own VIII. Caius had some members of the University water polo team and they drew me, firstly into water polo, and then into the swimming team. Both were rather Cinderella sports in those days, and we had to train at the Leys pool, since the only official University swimming facility was a stretch of the upper river, where costumes were reportedly optional – we did play a game or two there, but never in the nick. As I recall we defeated Oxford in swimming and water polo, both in 1972 and in 1973, and I was awarded my Blue and half-Blue for water polo. We also did pretty well in the British Universities' swimming, and our men's relay teams came away with a gold, a silver and a bronze.

I also found myself coaching the University Ladies' VIII, to my great delight. Helen McFie and Lina Talbot, both members of Darwin, were in that crew, and in fact

JOHN APPLEYARD

I was a keen, if rather inexpert, chess player, and I remember losing heavily against players such as Ray Keene and Bill Hartston, who were already among the leading players in the country. I fared little better against other Darwin players, and I remember many losses against Ole Bay-Petersen and others, including a very strong player from Azerbaijan (whose name I can't recall). Understandably, he preferred to play for money, but I fear he ran out of willing takers rather quickly. I remember taking him along to the University Chess Club, in the hope that he would find better qualified opposition there.

I fared rather better at rowing, partly because I was fortunate enough to share a boat with some great athletes, and partly because we were in far too low a division. In the 1972 May Races, the Darwin 1st boat won its oars. Our crew, as recorded in the CUBC programme, comprised Harold Lowe, Brian Christie, Richard Lysons, myself, Rob Wallace, John Lumley, Richard Melrose, Brian Morrisey and Rob Backus. We had previously missed our oars because, on one day, all the boats in front of us had bumped or been bumped, so for these races, we decided to concentrate on speed off the start. The strategy worked, and I don't think we rowed as many as 100 strokes in the entire four days.

Lina rowed in our successful 1973 Darwin crew in the May Bumps. Helen, a fellow African from Kenya, went on to great achievements in the rowing world. I quote her:

*I got the half-Blue in 1970–1 for beating Oxford and the full Blue in 1971–2 for winning every race we entered, including a couple at the national level. Lina also got the full Blue that year, but she was not a member of Darwin at the time, she was still in Newnham. She joined Darwin later, when she*

***Above and right:*** *A triumphant Darwin football team, 1983.*

*went on to study medicine. I was also President of the CU Women's Boat Club 1971–2. And I was on the British rowing team 1975 and was spare for the Olympic team in 1976. In 1980 I was the US Masters champion in the single and in 1991 won the FISA Veterans World Championships in the single and in the quad. I ended up rowing for 23 years and it all began at Darwin in 1970!*

Maarten de Wit was also, I believe, a hockey Blue in 1972, making it a vintage year for Darwin sport. Helen recalls that he may also have played squash for the University, being 'a fantastic squash player'.

### Plate Tectonics
#### Simon Loughe

When Darwin College was a mere 19 years old, its fledgling sports teams had yet to win a University competition. In January of 1983, the football team faced something of a dilemma. It had been drawn to play Downing College in the first round of Cuppers, at a time when Downing boasted no fewer than four Blues in their side. Being worldly-wise graduate types, the Football Committee members decided against a brief and possibly embarrassing 'run' in Cuppers, and voted instead to use an option open exclusively to teams from colleges with only one XI to their name, as we were then. This meant

we could choose to play either in Cuppers or in the Plate competition, which was open to all 2nd and lower XIs, *and* to colleges like us with only one team. So we entered the Plate, and left Downing to issue loud sighs of relief.

I was drafted in to replace the first-choice goalkeeper after our first two matches. After three further group games, we coasted into the quarter-finals, to resoundingly beat Pembroke 2nd XI away. We went on to the semi-final at home against, ironically, Downing 'Rugby' XI, who were fielding several rugby Blues, and who played an odd style

*Darwin football team, 1973–4.*

of lateral passing football, as well as snarling a lot, none of which worked, as we won 2–1. We were helped by their Blues scrum-half being sent off for some ill-timed kung fu practice on one of our midfielders in the second half.

And so we advanced to the final, played only three days later at Trinity College sports ground, on Friday 4 March. Our bruising semi-final didn't count against us, and I watched the game almost in splendid isolation as we pounded the Emmanuel College 2nd XI for 90 minutes,

on a glorious spring evening, without scoring. A good crowd had gathered, and they roared their support for both teams, but had to make do with our goal-bound efforts striking the Emma posts and crossbar, being cleared off the line by defenders, or being saved by their goalkeeper. Emma managed one shot, in the very last minute, that was deflected off a defender's shin, veered sharply to my right and, to my great relief, rolled inches wide of the post.

## DARWIN BASKETBALL CLUB

Trying to remember when Darwin Basketball Club was founded is really a hard job, although the women's team was created in 2000. The men's team has been around longer than the memories of the current members and the club brings quite a lot of success for Darwin, especially from the women's side.

The men's team, with captain Radu Rapiteanu, are currently in the first division and doing well. The first division is definitely tough, but there are good chances for the team to try and win the College league thanks to the coach, Benny Cheung (currently in his 12th year as an active member of Darwin Basketball Club). In 2012, indeed, the run towards league victory was only stopped very close to the finals, with an amazing game by the team.

The women's team has an outstandingly successful history. Just going around the bar it is possible to see year-by-year pictures of the team winning the college league.

Since 2008, the team has failed to win the league only once, in 2012, when it nonetheless reached the final. The captain in 2012–13 is Nittai Madrid, who has been the protagonist of most of the victories of recent years, and the team is now coached by Marco Zaccaria, helped by Ben Watts, after many years of work by Nils Grabole.

Both men's and women's teams tend also to share some social activities, and usually there are at least three events a year: an informal dinner before Christmas, a formal dinner during Easter term to celebrate the victories and a final barbecue held in July.

*Marco Zaccaria*

*Darwin College basketball teams, 2013.*

## DARWIN COLLEGE CRICKET CLUB

The Darwin College Cricket Club has been around for most of the College's history, but unfortunately records of the club's activities have been restricted to annual team photographs from the early 1990s until about 2006–7. For the short period for which there are records, Darwin College has excelled in the MCR Cricket League, winning the league in 2008–9 and 2010–11, and reaching the finals in 2009–10. This is a remarkable achievement, given that the club's primary focus is not on winning, but on making sure that as many Darwinians as possible are introduced to the sport, and get a chance to play it competitively. The club also prides itself on its inclusiveness, and has fielded mixed gender teams in every single match it has played (including friendly games) for at least the last four seasons (and possibly more).

*Mark D'Souza*

I had only played an extra-time period once before, as an outfield player, and remember being too tired to pass the half-way line at any point, so I watched in admiration as my teammates threw themselves at Emma once more. We won the match with a piece of brilliance from our centre forward, Jorge, who, with his back to goal nearly 40 yards out, somehow managed to turn and hit the ball from a throw-in, to send it arcing straight in to the top corner of the goal. It was truly a goal fit to win any final, and I can still see it like it was yesterday. We held out for a 1–0 win, and I have never wished precious seconds of my life to pass so quickly before or since.

We later heard our team was toasted in Hall that night not once, but twice. We had truly arrived!

Our team picture still hangs in the bar. As we had no goalkeeper's shirt, I had to use my tracksuit top in games instead, and you can't tell by looking, but the night before the photo shoot, I unscrewed each of my boot studs and cleaned them until they gleamed! That team was a really good footballing side, and I do wonder how we might have fared against Downing 1st XI had we taken them on.

## DRAMA
### Hugh Mellor

When I became a Fellow in 1971, Darwin was not an easy place to put on plays. In the Dining Hall, the only practicable indoor venue, there was no stage lighting and no proper stage. A small acting area with a simple set could indeed be set up opposite the entrance. But with no backstage area, and the Entertaining Room the only dressing room, performers had to enter and exit through the audience. And for many of the audience, ranged along the dining tables, and sideways on to an unraised stage, those entrances and exits were often the most visible parts of a show, especially when the performance required actors to sit or lie down.

Nor could we easily make plays more visible by staging them in the round in the centre of the hall. Not because we had to put the dining tables against the walls and rearrange all the chairs: that was manageable, even if the consequent delay tempted diners to seek postprandial entertainment elsewhere. The real problem was lighting.

127

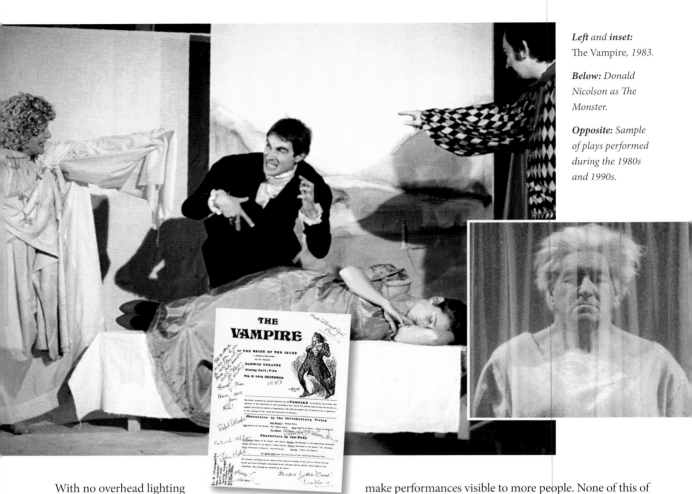

*Left and inset:*
The Vampire, *1983.*

*Below: Donald
Nicolson as The
Monster.*

*Opposite: Sample
of plays performed
during the 1980s
and 1990s.*

With no overhead lighting
bars, stage lights could
only be mounted on floor stands which, since they
had to be set aside for meals, had to be replaced, re-angled
and re-focused for each performance. More seriously still,
they couldn't be high enough to downlight a central stage
without blinding the surrounding audience.

Two innovations solved some of these problems.
One was the lighting bars that still top the Dining Hall
walls, with movable spotlights on them that can be placed,
angled and focused as required. Sockets for these are
wired to sockets in the alcove by the Hall entrance, where
a portable console can be used to design and run lighting
plots. The other, which alleviated the sightline problem,
was the acquisition of stage blocks to form raised stages to
make performances visible to more people. None of this of
course made Darwin Hall a proper theatre. It couldn't be
blacked out; there were still no proper dressing rooms, nor
anywhere to prepare or store sets, props or costumes; and
performances fitted round meals inevitably entail a tedious
shuffling of tables and chairs, and a small, ill-furnished stage
with little if any wing or backstage space.

What Darwin drama needs is an auditorium
which, like Robinson's, is as well-designed for plays and
concerts as for lectures. There need be no lack of good
plays to put in it, judging by the list opposite, ranging
from Chekhov (*The Bear* and *The Proposal*) to *Lord of the
Rings* (sic!). All of these productions were staged in the
Hall except for *Aria da Capo*, staged in the Old Library,
and *A Midsummer Night's Dream* and *The Tempest*, in

the garden. *The Dream* I recall especially: a magical production in June 1990, with the audience seated in a circle between the Hall and the copper beech while the action went on all round them.

The only other productions I remember as vividly, because I was involved in them, were done in the 1980s. Some were shorts, staged within mainly musical entertainments, like Stoppard's ten-minute abridgement of *Hamlet* in Darwin's 1982 May Week concert, and Shaw's *How He Lied to Her Husband* in the 1983 concert. Others were longer, like a captivating 1985 adaptation of part of *Winnie the Pooh*, directed by François Penz, whose characters, in an urban setting, were not animals but people. But for me the highlights of 1980s Darwin drama were two plays from *The Hour of One*, a collection of Gothic melodramas published in 1975. One was the 1986 production of H.M. Milner's 1826 adaptation of Mary Shelley's 1818 *Frankenstein*, featuring a green-lit monster behind a gauze, melodramatic acting to match, and a

| Date | Month | Days | Date | Title |
|------|-------|------|------|-------|
| 1985 | Mar | W, F | 13, 15 | *Winnie the Pooh* |
| 1986 | Feb | W, F | 19, 21 | *The Fate of Frankenstein* |
| 1987 | Dec | W–F | 4–6 | *The Gypsy's Revenge* |
| 1988 | Mar | W–F | 2–4 | *The Castle Spectre* |
| 1989 | Mar | W–F | 1–3 | *Lysistrata* |
| 1990 | Mar | W–F | 7–9 | *The Bear* and *The Proposal* |
| | Jun | W–Sa | 20–23 | *A Midsummer Night's Dream* |
| | Nov | Tu–Sa | 6–10 | *The Persians* |
| 1992 | May | W–F | 6–8 | *The Marriage of Figaro* |
| 1993 | Mar | W–F | 24–6 | *The Real Thing* |
| 1994 | Dec | M–W | 5–7 | *Mandragola* |
| 1996 | May | Th–Sa | 9–11 | *Aria da Capo* |
| | Dec | Th–Sa | 5–7 | *The Physicists* |
| 1997 | Dec | W–Th | 3–4 | *Dogg's Hamlet* |
| 1998 | Jun | Th–F | 18–19 | *Lord of the Rings* |
| | Nov | M–Th | 23–6 | *A Man for All Seasons* |
| 1999 | Feb | Th–Su | 25–8 | *Amadeus* |
| | Jun | Tu–Sa | 15–19 | *The Tempest* |

brilliant realisation (on the Hall's balcony) of as much as was safely feasible of the final stage directions:

*The Monster ... rushes up to the apex of the mountain [Etna] – the Soldiery rush in and fire on him – he immediately leaps into the Crater, now vomiting burning lava, and the Curtain falls.*

The other, three years earlier, was of J.R. Planché's 1820 *The Vampire*, or *The Bride of the Isles*, set in Scotland, and predating Bram Stoker's *Dracula* by 77 years. That too, as the picture opposite shows, had satisfyingly over-the-top acting.

A projected production of *Dracula* itself nearly followed in 1995, but in the end didn't, prompting Donald Nicolson, to whom Darwin drama owes so much, not only as an actor, but as a lighting designer, set builder and archivist, to an elegy:

*Iste comes notus, qui non – sic fabula dicta –*
*umquam mortem obiit, Dracula vivit adhuc,*
*mox surrecturus per scaenam Darwinianam*
*ut nostri actores drama iterum facient?*
*Nam credebamus vivum illum etiam bene habentem*
*esse in Purfleeto. Non tamen est ita. Vae?*
*Quae ratio est? Tandem est caesus vereque sepultus.*
*Fixa Apathia sudis lignea pectori inest.*

(Does Dracula still live, that famous count who – so the story is told – has not ever met death, soon to rise again on the stage of Darwin, when our actors once again perform a play? For we believed he was still alive and well in Purfleet. It is not so, however. Alas! What is the reason? At last he has been slain and truly buried. The wooden stake of Apathy lies fixed in his breast.)

Donald's elegy proved depressingly prophetic, since apathy killed off Darwin drama too at the end of the last century, since when it has produced no new productions. It will be a sad reflection on a once-cultured graduate community if today's Darwinians fail to revive the proud tradition of drama recorded in the table (left).

## THE DARWIN COLLEGE BAR
### Michael Hoenig (1996–2004)

The two things that defined my time at Darwin the most were: my PhD in astronomy and the College bar. But not necessarily in that order.

Darwin's bar is quite unique in that it is one of the last student-run college bars in Cambridge, meaning it is staffed – and run – entirely by student volunteers. Since there is no need to make a profit, the prices tend to be lower than in pubs.

It also provides a great opportunity to socialise with fellow students.

I signed up for bar shifts during my first year at College. I must have come across as rather keen (meaning, I spent a lot of my evenings there). After about a year I got asked to join the Bar Committee, which is a core group of about 6–8 people who are involved in the day-to-day running of the bar. My first job was cleaning the beer pipes; this would be done every Sunday, often to the soundtrack of one of the bands playing 'music' in the common room. I eventually moved on to taking care of the weekly orders of beer, before I graduated to being the bar's treasurer. The following year I became the Secretary (dealing mostly with staff and related issues) and a while later I ended up being crowned bar Chair.

So by now it should have become pretty clear that the bar, and the people working it, were my constant companions (and occasional distractions) during my time in Cambridge. No doubt everyone reading this will be reminded of their own little anecdotes, their own experiences of Cambridge's best college bar. I think for me the highlights would not just be the big events (like the annual Oktoberfest, for example – in November – that has been going strong for close to a decade now), but also those quiet nights when you just needed to unwind a little over a pint, and you could be sure to come across a friendly face to chat with for a while. I knew a number of students who weren't living on-site and who would like to come in occasionally and 'touch base' with their College … what better place to do this than at the bar?

At times we almost became victims of our own popularity – some nights the bar would be absolutely packed with people, which was an issue due to the fact that we are a 'members only' bar, meaning we are only allowed to serve Darwinians and their guests (anyone remember that perennial favourite, the 'signing-in book'?) And I would be lying if I said we never had run-ins with the College authorities due to things like noise, broken glass or occasional graffiti.

But the folks running the bar are a pretty responsible and adaptable bunch, which is why the bar has remained open (most of the time), successful (a lot of the time) and a pretty good place to go for a drink, throughout all these years.

This is mostly just a fond memory for me now, but every time I come back to Cambridge I look forward to popping into the bar and letting my mind drift back to the days when my fellow bar-staffers became something of a replacement family for me. As I noticed after leaving Darwin, having bar work on your CV tends to count as a pretty big bonus when it comes to social skills – if you can turn away a group of ten drunken football players at closing time, you can handle pretty much any situation your job might throw at you.

Remember, former Darwinians are always welcome, so come and have a pint of beer, a glass of wine, or maybe even sample one of our 20-odd single malts next time you're in town!

Once a Darwinian …

## BRIDGING THE DISTANCE
### Geta Dumitriu

Arriving from Bucharest on a greyish day, I got out of a cab in front of Darwin College. That same evening I became familiar with one of its frequent manifestations. As I was still a kiddie by age in 1971, the College took on for the occasion the features of a benevolent hostess. Introducing herself as Sylvia Fitton Jackson, the Associate Dean somehow conveyed to me the message that it wouldn't be long before I got rid of my complexes and felt

*Covers of* River Rat, *the student magazine named in honour of Gwen Raverat.*

at home in the new community. Lively encouragement also came from a fair-haired young scholar sitting opposite me at the table. Little could I guess then that in Evelyne Hanquart I would have a close friend, not only during my stay at Darwin, but also for decades to come. Her friendship has helped me a lot in my personal life and has also become professionally fruitful since Romania broke with the totalitarian regime. Our English departments – hers at the Sorbonne, mine at Bucharest University – have developed an exchange programme from which members of the teaching staff and students, mostly Romanians, have been benefiting all these years.

My circle of friends and acquaintants enlarged as daily life made for togetherness. A new experience for me was the company and conversation of the Fellows: at dinners, either formal in the Dining Hall, or informal and friendly when offered on Sundays in the Fellows' own cosy homes. They also would hand to those interested food for thought in a different wrapper. There is still stored in a safe corner of my memory the warm and open-minded atmosphere created by their evening lectures, the body language of their speech often undermining received notions of the famous English self-possession. However, not all of them betrayed such an emotional nature as Professor Graham Hough, who was unable to suppress his tears in the talk he gave about an Asian country whose people enchanted him in many ways.

Just as the Associate Dean predicted, it did not take me long to get a sense of belonging to Darwin. On returning to Romania I carried with me precious memories: of the grounds by the River Cam; of feeding the ducks with Franca; of the tall tree whose crown I often contemplated from the dormer of my room; of the Sundays when it was my turn to serve tea to my colleagues; of the irrepressible feeling I had that I was simply going home whenever I turned the corner into Silver Street after doing my reading in the UL, visiting other colleges, or listening in King's to the illuminating and inspiring talk of my supervisor, Tony Tanner. And, animating all these figures in their frames, is a spirit bridging distances between humans wherever they are or come from.

## A GLOBAL COMMUNITY
### Donna Seto-Young (1976–9)

I was accommodated in Darwin College for one year, and for two years at 18 Guest Road. I still have fond memories of my days there, especially the wonderful friendships that were nurtured. Moreover, the excellent training I received at Darwin College has served me well in my career path.

In 1977 I had a small, private wedding in Cambridge. My supervisor, Professor David Ellar, and Dr Elisabeth Leedham-Green were my witnesses. After my marriage Darwin College offered me a flat in Eltisley Avenue.

While I lived in Darwin College, I met Annamaria Simonazzi and Cathleen Sullivan. Dr Simonazzi is a Professor of Economics at the University of Rome La Sapienza, while Dr Sullivan is currently a pathologist. I also met Janice Crimp, Mark Lawrence, Anthony Weidberg, Timothy Smithers, Bruce Wiltshire and Rose Zamoyska in 18 Guest Road. In addition, I worked together with Andreas Freiburghaus in the same laboratory at the Biochemistry Department.

After I graduated from Darwin College, I was able to reunite with a few old College friends. During my two-year postdoctoral study at Harvard University School of Medicine I saw Drs Simonazzi, Sullivan and Zamoyska. It

**Above:** *The copper beech in autumn.*     **Above right:** *Christmas at Darwin.*     **Opposite:** *Chart showing country of origin of Darwin students.*

was a pleasure to meet Annamaria Simonazzi, especially as she had travelled all the way from Italy to see me and Cathleen Sullivan. We enjoyed our experiences and companionships at Darwin College. I also encountered Marwin K. Al-Shawi in several scientific meetings. Dr Al-Shawi and I shared a common interest in ATP synthase. Currently he is working on catalytic and transport cycles of ABC exporters.

While living in New York, I met Dr Roger Groden, who worked at Cornell University School of Medicine. We share the same interest in my current research, the role of insulin resistance effect on ovarian function. We often have lunches and dinners together, sharing our pleasant memories of Darwin College. Roger Groden is retired and currently resides in Virginia with his lovely wife. My colleague Andreas Freiburghaus is working in the University Hospital of Zurich as Head of Data Management for the hospital's webpage. Anthony

Weidberg is working at CERN and is a tutor and Fellow at St John's College, Oxford.

The friendships that I have made at Darwin College will always hold a special place in my heart. I can truly call my colleagues – whom I have grown to revere – my family. The experience that I have gained from Darwin changed me as a whole. I understood the value of friendships and family that I will always carry with me in the future.

## A LITTLE PIECE OF CANADA
### Della Wilkinson

Darwin has many special memories for me; most notably it is the place where I met the man who became my husband, Steve Zan. There were many weddings that resulted from those three years spent enjoying coffee in the Parlour or under the magnificent copper beech in the warmer months, and many of them, like ours, involved cross-cultural unions.

| | 1968 | 1973 | 1978 | 1983 | 1988 | 1993 | 1998 | 2003 | 2008 | 2012 |
|---|---|---|---|---|---|---|---|---|---|---|
| UK | 49 | 136 | 188 | 196 | 209 | 221 | 217 | 281 | 206 | 219 |
| Albania | | | | | | | 1 | 1 | | |
| Argentina | | | 1 | | | | 2 | | 3 | 1 |
| Armenia | | | | | | | 1 | 1 | | |
| Australia | 2 | 10 | 11 | 5 | 9 | 4 | 6 | 11 | 3 | 12 |
| Austria | | 1 | 1 | | | | | 4 | 6 | 5 |
| Azerbaijan | — | — | — | — | — | | | | 1 | 1 |
| Bahamas | | | | | | | 1 | | | |
| Bangladesh | | 2 | | | 2 | | 2 | 2 | 2 | 3 |
| Barbados | 1 | | 1 | | | 1 | 1 | | | |
| Belarus | — | — | — | — | — | | 1 | 2 | 1 | 2 |
| Belgium | | | 2 | | | 3 | 3 | 1 | | 7 |
| Bolivia | | | | 1 | | | | | | 1 |
| Bosnia | — | — | — | — | — | | 1 | 1 | | |
| Botswana | | | | | | 1 | | | | |
| Brazil | 2 | 3 | 3 | 5 | 3 | 3 | 2 | 4 | 7 | 6 |
| Bulgaria | | | | | | | 1 | 1 | | |
| Burma | | 1 | | | | | | | | |
| Canada | 5 | 13 | 21 | 8 | 14 | 16 | 19 | 15 | 16 | 23 |
| Chile | 1 | 1 | | | 2 | | 2 | 2 | 5 | 9 |
| China | | | | 4 | 10 | 12 | 12 | 20 | 51 | 41 |
| China (Taiwan) | | | 1 | 4 | 3 | 11 | 6 | 5 | 3 | 2 |
| Colombia | | | | | | 1 | | | | 1 |
| Croatia | — | — | — | — | — | 1 | 2 | 1 | 3 | 3 |
| Cyprus | | | 3 | | | 1 | 4 | 4 | 5 | 1 |
| Czechoslovakia | 1 | 1 | | | | — | — | — | | |
| Czech Republic | — | — | — | — | — | | | | 1 | 4 |
| Denmark | 2 | 3 | 1 | 4 | 2 | 1 | 6 | 7 | 3 | 2 |
| Ecuador | | | 1 | | | | 1 | | 1 | 1 |
| Egypt | | 1 | 2 | 3 | 1 | 1 | 1 | 1 | 2 | 2 |
| Eire | | 3 | | | 3 | | 1 | 14 | 12 | 18 |
| Estonia | — | — | — | — | — | 1 | | | | |
| Ethiopia | 1 | 1 | | | | | | | | |
| Fiji | | | | | | 1 | | | | |
| Finland | | 1 | 1 | 1 | 1 | | | 4 | 1 | 1 |
| France | | 2 | 2 | 3 | 1 | 5 | 7 | 9 | 10 | 14 |
| Gambia | | | | | 1 | | | | | |
| Germany | | 2 | 4 | 5 | 8 | 18 | 27 | 24 | 41 | 60 |
| Ghana | | | | | 1 | | 1 | 1 | 1 | 1 |
| Greece | 1 | 7 | 6 | 7 | 5 | 8 | 9 | 21 | 12 | 9 |
| Honduras | | 1 | | | | | | | | |
| Hong Kong | 1 | 3 | 3 | 5 | 7 | 8 | 2 | 3 | | 8 |
| Hungary | 1 | | | | | 1 | 1 | | 2 | 2 |
| Iceland | | 1 | 1 | 2 | | | 1 | | 2 | 2 |
| India | 1 | 3 | 3 | 1 | 17 | 13 | 6 | 8 | 16 | 18 |
| Iran | | 1 | 2 | 2 | 6 | 1 | | | 4 | 3 |
| Iraq | | | 3 | 3 | | | | | | |
| Israel | | 1 | 2 | 2 | 1 | 1 | 2 | 7 | | 2 |
| Italy | 2 | 7 | 7 | 9 | 5 | 12 | 11 | 6 | 13 | 11 |
| Jamaica | | | | | | 1 | | 1 | | |
| Japan | | 2 | 9 | 14 | 2 | 8 | 13 | 7 | 9 | 3 |
| Jordan | | 1 | | 2 | 1 | | | | | |
| Kazakhstan | — | — | — | — | — | | | | 1 | 1 |
| Kenya | | 1 | | | 3 | 2 | 1 | 1 | 1 | 1 |
| Korea (South) | | | | 4 | 2 | 4 | 8 | | 6 | 6 |
| Kosovo | — | — | — | — | — | | 1 | | | |
| Kuwait | | | | 1 | | | | | | |
| Kyrgyzstan | — | — | — | — | — | | | | | 1 |
| Latvia | — | — | — | — | — | | | | | 1 |

| | 1968 | 1973 | 1978 | 1983 | 1988 | 1993 | 1998 | 2003 | 2008 | 2012 |
|---|---|---|---|---|---|---|---|---|---|---|
| Lebanon | 1 | | | 1 | 1 | | 1 | 1 | | |
| Lesotho | | | | | | | | 1 | | |
| Libya | | | 1 | | | | | | | |
| Lithuania | — | — | — | — | — | | | | 1 | 1 |
| Luxembourg | | | 1 | | | | | | | |
| Macedonia | — | — | — | — | — | | 2 | 1 | 1 | |
| Malawi | | | | | | | 2 | | 3 | |
| Malaysia | 1 | 1 | | 4 | 2 | 9 | 7 | 6 | 2 | 8 |
| Malta | 1 | | | | | 1 | 2 | | | |
| Mauritius | | 1 | | | | | | 1 | | 1 |
| Mexico | | 4 | 4 | 1 | 2 | 4 | 4 | 2 | 6 | 17 |
| Morocco | | | | | | | | | | 1 |
| Nepal | | | | | | | | 1 | | |
| Netherlands | | 1 | 1 | 1 | 2 | 3 | 2 | 1 | 5 | 14 |
| New Zealand | 2 | 4 | 2 | 5 | 6 | 9 | 3 | 5 | 4 | 10 |
| Nigeria | 2 | 3 | | 2 | 5 | 3 | | 4 | 1 | 1 |
| Norway | | | | | | 1 | 1 | | 1 | 2 |
| Oman | | | | | | | | 1 | | |
| Pakistan | 4 | | 2 | 3 | 6 | 4 | 6 | 1 | | 5 |
| Palestine | | | | | | | 1 | | | |
| Peru | | 1 | | 2 | | | | 1 | 2 | 1 |
| Philippines | | | 1 | | | | 2 | 1 | | |
| Poland | 1 | 1 | | 1 | | | 2 | 1 | 3 | 10 |
| Portugal | 1 | 4 | 2 | 4 | | 2 | 6 | 8 | 9 | 10 |
| Romania | | | | | | | | 1 | 1 | 4 |
| Russia | | | | | | | 1 | 3 | 4 | 5 |
| Saint Kitts | | | | | | | | 1 | | |
| Saint Lucia | | | | | | 1 | | | | |
| Saudi Arabia | 1 | 1 | | 1 | 1 | | | | | |
| Senegal | | | | | | | 1 | | | |
| Serbia | | | | | | | 1 | | 1 | 1 |
| Sierra Leone | | | | 1 | | | | | | |
| Singapore | | | | | | 5 | 6 | 3 | 3 | 9 |
| Slovakia | — | — | — | — | — | | | 1 | | |
| Slovenia | — | — | — | — | — | | | | | 1 |
| South Africa | 4 | 4 | | 2 | 1 | 4 | 8 | 3 | 4 | 1 |
| Spain | | 2 | | | 1 | 1 | 2 | 8 | 4 | 12 |
| Sri Lanka | 1 | 1 | | 2 | 1 | 2 | 1 | 3 | 2 | 2 |
| Sudan | 1 | | | 1 | | | | 1 | | |
| Sweden | 1 | 1 | 2 | | 2 | | 3 | 1 | 2 | 6 |
| Switzerland | | 2 | 3 | 1 | | | 1 | | 2 | 4 |
| Syria | | 1 | | | | 1 | | | | 1 |
| Thailand | | 2 | 1 | 2 | | 5 | 6 | 5 | 7 | 5 |
| Trinidad | | | | | | 1 | 1 | 1 | | |
| Turkey | | | 1 | 3 | 2 | 0 | 2 | | 3 | 5 |
| Uganda | | 3 | | 1 | 1 | | 1 | | | |
| Ukraine | — | — | — | — | — | | 1 | 2 | | 1 |
| Uruguay | | 1 | | 1 | 1 | | | | | |
| USA | 17 | 22 | 25 | 18 | 24 | 25 | 29 | 32 | 45 | 39 |
| USSR | | 1 | | | | — | — | — | — | — |
| Venezuela | 1 | | 1 | 2 | | | 1 | 1 | | 1 |
| Vietnam | | | | | | | | | 1 | 2 |
| Yemen | | | | | | | | | | 1 |
| Yugoslavia | 1 | | | | | | | | | |
| Zaire | | | 1 | 1 | | | | | | |
| Zambia | | 1 | | | | | | 1 | | |
| Zimbabwe | | | 1 | | | 2 | 1 | 1 | | |
| **TOTAL** | **110** | **257** | **330** | **344** | **387** | **446** | **493** | **567** | **582** | **688** |

*Elisabeth Leedham-Green rehearsing students for their graduation ceremony, 2012.*

For my first Christmas at Darwin in 1987 I was living off-site in a suburban house with a large and unkempt garden that contained several Christmas trees (now that I have lived in Canada for 22 years I can identify them as pine and fir trees). I was just getting to know the Canadian who lived around the corner from me when one December evening at the College bar we ended up volunteering to bring in a Christmas tree for the DCSA. It was an early introduction to Canadian living, when Steve turned up a few nights later with a hand saw and we cut down one of the small trees in my back garden. The only mode of transport available was my Mini Cooper, so under the cover of darkness we wedged the tree into the back seat with the tip facing towards the windshield. Suddenly the small tree seemed rather large, and it was impossible to see my passenger as I sped through the streets of Cambridge. Unfortunately our planning was not great, as we had tickets to watch Ben Elton perform at the Corn Exchange that evening and we did not leave enough time to drop off the tree before the show. Ben Elton put on a great show and it was several hours before we left the Exchange to find the inside windows of the car encrusted with ice crystals. Now it was Steve's turn for some cultural education, when he asked if I could get the ice-scraper from the trunk! We managed to carve out port-holes using credit cards, which provided sufficient vision to drive the short distance to Darwin. Needless to say, the car smelled very fresh for many months afterwards.

### 'ONCE A DARWINIAN, ALWAYS A DARWINIAN'

**Mihirinie Wijayawardene, DCSA President, 1999–2000**

The September that I arrived at Darwin I was placed in temporary accommodation until the College found me more permanent digs. The box room at Summerfield was neither the best introduction to Cambridge nor to Darwin, and my new laboratory certainly did nothing to dispel the Oxbridge stereotypes that I'd hoped were just that. Luckily, I was soon moved to Gwen Raverat House, just as the Freshers' events at Darwin were kicking into gear, and I quickly found my place in College and in Cambridge.

The year I joined Darwin, its student body represented around 56 countries of the world and it had its highest intake, to date, of female students (this figure continued to grow over the next few years). Women were also strongly represented on the Darwin College Student Association (DCSA); in fact, during my time in Cambridge, there were more female than male DCSA Presidents. I never felt like a minority or a second-class citizen at Darwin, and in my experience, if ever a student needed support, they got it.

There were many things I loved about Darwin: the Old Granary (and in particular watching the sun rise over the river), the island (which hosted countless barbecues on balmy summer evenings), the magnificent copper beech tree in the garden, the fact that we were only one of seven colleges through which the River Cam ran, night punting, the annual lecture series and the lack of a high table at Formal Hall. But the very best thing about Darwin College, for me, was its multi-ethnic, multi-cultural, diverse student body that brought together an eclectic mix of characters and disciplines under one roof. Being a graduate college made a huge difference, too. It meant that the students joining Darwin every year brought with them their own individual viewpoints and life experiences from a vast array of backgrounds and universities, both domestic and foreign.

At the Welcome Dinner I attended when I first joined the College, the Dean, Dr Leo Howe, told us newcomers that once we became Darwinians, no matter where we went from there, we would forever be Darwinians – and I've always felt this statement to be true.

*Graduation, 2012.*

# LIST OF SUBSCRIBERS

**This book has been made possible through the generosity of the following subscribers**

| | | | | | |
|---|---|---|---|---|---|
| Adrian Fellow | AF | Fellow | F | Microsoft Fellow | MiF |
| Charles and Katharine | | Finley Research Fellow | FRF | Munby Fellow | MF |
| Darwin Research Fellow | CKDRF | Founding Fellow | FF | Research Fellow | RF |
| Darwin Family | DF | Honorary Fellow | HF | Schlumberger Fellow | SF |
| Emerita Status | ES | Master | M | Vice-Master | V-M |
| Emeritus Fellow | EF | Master Emeritus | ME | Visiting Member | VM |

| | | | | | |
|---|---|---|---|---|---|
| Dr Anna a Campo | 1984 | Ole Bay-Petersen | 1973 | Dr Lawson W. Brigham | 1997 |
| Dr Michael Addison | 1968 | Benjamin P. Bedard | 2000 | Peter Brindle | F and Bursar (2001) |
| Dr Michael A. Ainslie | 1981 | Andrew Beharrell and | | Rebecca Brodie | 2001 |
| Professor Michael Akam | F (2006) | Dr Diana Beharrell | 1982; 1982 | Dr Wendy Brooks | 2000 |
| Emma Algotsson | 1996 | Matthew Bell | 1997 | Professor Willy Brown | M (2000); ME (2012) |
| Dr Shazeeda Ali | 1994 | Amy Bellman Davis | 1994 | Dr Christian Bryant | 1991 |
| Zainun Ali | 1984 | Professor Martin H. Belsky | 1968 | Dr James William Buckie | 1983 |
| Tiago Maranhão Alves | 2001 | Dr Derek Bendall | F (1965); EF (1997) | Angela Linge Budiarso | 2001 |
| Dr Lisa Francesca Andermann | 1991 | Dr Andreas Bender | 2003 | Sir Arnold Burgen | M (1982); HF (1989) |
| Dr Mike Anderson | 1977 | Dr Amanda Benjamin (née Hibell) | 1996 | Professor Lars Burman | 1986 |
| Siew-Mun Ang | 1992 | Professor Walter Bernhart | 1973 | | |
| Dr Jannis Angelis | 2000 | Dr Tamás Bertényi | 1997 | Juan I.C. Canseco-Gomez | 1994 |
| Mohammad-Irfan Arif | 2010 | Professor Carluccio Bianchi | 1973 | Dr Stephen C. Capsaskis | 1981 |
| Dr Sharon Ashbrook | CKDRF (2003) | Dr Christopher M. Bishop | F (1998) | Carlos Alberto Carbajo-Martinez | 1995 |
| Dr Graham Ashley | 1980 | Dr Alan Blackwell | 1995; F (2001) | Jonathan Cardenas | 2007 |
| Tomiya Atsumi | 1977 | Dr David Blagden | AF (2012) | Dr Joseph W. Carnwath | 1976 |
| Luxmon Attapich | 1992 | Michael Blank | 2004 | Dr Philip Carr Ashworth | RF (2010) |
| Faisal Azim | 2011 | Dr Peter Blustin and Dr Mary Blustin | | Professor Robin Carrell | 1965 |
| | | | 1969; 1969 | Bernard Cazenove | HF (2005) |
| Dr Tanya Bagrij | 1996 | I.L. Bondy | 1988 | Cynthia Malini Celestine | 1983 |
| Khadija Alia Bah | 1999 | Professor Robert Borland | EF (1967) | Dr Bernardo Ceriani | 1975 |
| Lily Bai | 2011 | Avery Borreliz | 2012 | Professor Amaresh Chakrabarti | 1987 |
| Dr Alex Bain and Dr Janet Rossant | 1972; 1972 | Dr Janine Bourriau | F (1983); EF (2008) | Dr Sammy L.I. Chan | 1980 |
| Dr Ali Sher Bajwa | 2004 | Sir John Bradfield | HF (1973) | Henry Hon Lam Chan | 1999 |
| Ian Banner | 1992 | Dr John K. Bradley | 1988 | Godfrey Chandler | HF (1978) |
| Charles C. Barlow Jr. | 1981 | Danielle Emma Bradshaw | 2010 | Dr Munawar Chaudhri | F (1990); EF (2009) |
| Dr W.T. Bartoszewski | 1980 | Dr Ian Braid and Dr Judith Braid (née Slater) | | Dr Jen-Hung Chen | 1993 |
| Dr Thomas (Geoff) Battye | 1999 | | 1968; 1966 | Claire Christmas | 2011 |
| Dr Jan Bay-Petersen | 1970 | Dr Nicholas Branson | F (1983); EF (2007) | Clement Chung | 1995 |

| | |
|---|---|
| Professor Giovanni Cianci | 1969 |
| Nicholas Becket Cipolla | 2000 |
| Dr Mike Clark | 1978 |
| Mrs C. Cocke in memory of | |
| Dr Thomas Cocke | F (1987) |
| Leo Cogin | 1997 |
| Dr Harlan K. Cohen | 1971 |
| Dr Graham Douglas Coley | 1968 |
| Dr Alison Collins | 1990 |
| Dr Margaret Cone | F (1992); EF (2013) |
| Dr John Cook | 1976 |
| Michael Cook | 1990 |
| Frances Cooley | 1978 |
| Professor John R. Cooper | F (1993); EF (2011) |
| Professor David Cornell | 1971 |
| Professor Amancio Costa Pinto | 1983 |
| Dr Carole A. Cotter | 1979 |
| Professor Russell Cowburn | F (2011) |
| Dr Nancy Cox | 1970 |
| Dr Tony Cox | F (1999); EF (2008) |
| Dr Barry Crosbie and | |
| Dr Sharanya Jayawickrama | 2000; 2000 |
| Andrew Cross | 1984 |
| Professor Christopher Cullen | |
| F (2005) and College Praelector | |
| Dr Mark Alexander Curran | MF (2011) |
| Dr Michael Czwarno | 1984 |
| | |
| Artur da Silvo Pinto and Rafaela da Silvo Pinto | |
| Friends of the Boat Club | |
| Rabia Dada | 2009 |
| Dr Martyn Dade-Robertson | 2001 |
| Sarah Dakshy (née Selby) | 1997 |
| Professor Giuseppe Dalessandro | 1973 |
| Angela Darwin | DF |
| Edward Darwin | DF |
| Dr Saroj Bala Datta | 1974 |
| Professor D. Ceri Davies | 1974 |
| Professor Peter Francis Davies | 1972 |
| Professor Philip Dawid | |
| 1966; F (2007); EF (2013) | |
| Dr Selvino de Kort | SF (2003) |
| Dr John de Pont | 1981 |
| Dr Mark de Rond | F (2006) |
| Dr Eric de Silva and Mrs Daniela de Silva | |
| (née Karadzovska) | 1997; 1998 |
| Dr Saulo Santos de Souza | 2007 |
| Professor Maarten de Wit | 1969 |
| Dr Mathias Deckers | 1991 |
| Dr Gabriel des Rosiers | 1988 |
| Dr Giuliano Di Bacco | MF (2005) |
| Dr Mario Di Gregorio | 1975 |
| Dr Peter Dickman | 1987 |
| Dr Sean Francis O'Brien Donaghey | 1969 |
| Stéphane Doyen | 2009 |
| Dr Daphne Fielding Drabble | 1966 |
| Dr Scott Drimie | 1996 |
| Dr Francis Drobniewski | 1983 |

| | |
|---|---|
| Samantha M.N. Dugas | 1995 |
| Dr Andreas Dullweber and | |
| Mrs Silvia Dullweber | 1995; 1995 |
| Dr Louisa Dunlop | 2003 |
| Dr Anna Elizabeth Dyer | 2000 |
| | |
| Dr Jenny Edmonds (née Gray) | 1968 |
| Dr Brita Elvevåg | 1992 |
| Dr Ulf Martin Engel | 1990 |
| Dr Richard Erskine | 1977 |
| | |
| Professor Andy Fabian | F (1983) |
| Dr Rosienne Farrugia | 2004 |
| Professor John Feather | MF (1977) |
| Dr Julie Fedor | RF (2011) |
| Dr David Allan Feller | 2005; RF (2010) |
| Professor Anne C. Ferguson-Smith | F (1997) |
| Anthony Fiske | 1971 |
| Dr Hugh Fleming and Mrs Julia Fleming | |
| F (1969); EF (1991); Benefactors | |
| Helen Foord | College Accountant |
| Alfred Alan Foster | 1997 |
| Professor C. Mary R. Fowler | 1972; M (2012) |
| Roger France | Invited Member (2000) |
| Dr Stephen Freeman | 1968 |
| Dr Sven Friedemann | SF (2011) |
| Dr Peter Friend | F (1974); EF (2001) |
| Dr Geeta Fuglevand | 1988 |
| Wai Lun Alan Fung | 2001 |
| | |
| Professor C. Giovanni Galizia | 1989 |
| Dr Jane Garnett | 1982 |
| Dr Ed Garratt | 1999 |
| Matthew Gasperetti | 2008 |
| Professor Denis Gauvreau | 1975 |
| Simon Geard | 1979 |
| Professor Paul Gibbs | 1997 |
| Janet Gibson | College Registrar |
| Dr Talat Mah Giddings | 1972 |
| Holger E. Giese | 1987 |
| Cheok Weng Goh | 1990 |
| Dr Andrew Marc Antony Goldfinch | 2007 |
| George Gömöri | F (1969); EF (2001) |
| Professor Roger Gosden | 1970 |
| Dr Nils Grabole | 2009 |
| Professor Maciej W. Grabski | 1969 |
| Dr Sarah L. Greaves | 1995 |
| Dr Hilary A.C. Green | 1996 |
| Zachary Green | 2003 |
| Professor Harald W. Griesshammer | 1990 |
| Dr Philip Grover | 1965 |
| Sigurdur R. Gudjonsson | 1975 |
| Francsico J. Guerra y Rullán | 1971 |
| | |
| Meredith Hagel | 2010 |
| Alison Hamley (née Holbrey) | 1989 |
| Professor Oliver Hankinson | 1969 |
| Dr Nerissa K. Hannink | 1999 |

| | |
|---|---|
| Dr Richard H.J. Hannink | 1970 |
| Professor Evelyne Hanquart-Turner | 1971 |
| Ian Hargrave | 1991 |
| Dr Brian Harney | 2004 |
| Dr Rob Harris | 1996 |
| Dr Tim Harrison and Dr Jenny Harrison | |
| 1969; 1971 | |
| Jorgen Haug | 2009 |
| Professor Dean Hawkes and | |
| Mrs Christine Hawkes | F (1976); EF (2005) |
| Jacqueline Hayhoe | ES |
| Professor Jonathan Luke Heeney | F (2012) |
| Jean Hélie | 2007 |
| Professor Paul Hellewell | 1980 |
| Dr Richard Henderson | F (1981); EF (2012) |
| Roger Heumann | 1997 |
| Dr J.D. Hill | 1987 |
| Mary Hill Harris | ES |
| Dr Raymond Hill and Mrs Nancy S. Hill | |
| 1977; 1977 | |
| Dianne Hinds | 2002 |
| Dr Michael Hoenig | 1996 |
| Dr Jessie Hohmann | RF (2009) |
| Professor Karl-J. Hölkeskamp | FRF (1987) |
| Dr Luke Holmes | 2000 |
| Jack Brian Hood | 1971 |
| Dr Yumi Horikane | 1996 |
| Peter K. Hosking | 2003 |
| Jim Howley | 1981 |
| Professor William W. Hsieh | 1981 |
| Dr David Hughes and Ms Evadné Grant | |
| 1984; 1986 | |
| Dr Iain Hutchison | 1979 |
| | |
| Dr Kazutoshi Ichikawa | 1994 |
| Dr Martin Iddon | 1998 |
| Dr Marco Iuliano | Research Associate (2009) |
| | |
| Barbara Janta | 2006 |
| Dr Ayal Jayatilaka | 1972 |
| Richard Jebb | 1987 |
| Dr Anita Jellings | 1976 |
| Yuri Ji | 2004 |
| Mo Jia | 2011 |
| Ao Jiang | 2005 |
| Stanley Lee Wai Jin | 2012 |
| Anders Steingrim Johnsen | 2007 |
| Dr Chris Johnson | HF (1978) |
| Dr L.H. Jones | 1987 |
| Professor Martin Jones | F (2001) and V-M |
| Andrew Jordan | 1972 |
| Dr Mark Joshi | F (1995) |
| | |
| Michael Anthony Kain | 1977 |
| Dr John Kamal | 1984 |
| Dr Venediktos Kapetanakis | 2008 |
| Dr Sreerama Karun | 1985 |
| Jordan I. Katz | 1981 |

| | | | | | |
|---|---|---|---|---|---|
| Dr Nikolas Kazantzis | 1997 | Yoichi Maeda | 1983 | Naabia Ofosu-Amaah | 2008 |
| Dr Peter Kearns | 1979 | Scott Magliochetti | 1988 | Shihoko Ogawa | 1999 |
| Dr Peter Kehoe | 1971 | Dr Diarmuid Maguire | | Professor Akira Ohira | VM (1990) |
| Alice Kelly | 2010 | Dr Thomas Manke | 1993 | Professor Sumie Okada | 1979 |
| Dr Séamas Kelly | 1993 | Dr Yseult Marique | 2006 | Professor Yayoi Okada | 2002 |
| Dr Warren Kerley | 2002 | Dr Peter D. Martin | 1976 | Brian Omotani | 1973 |
| Professor Stephen Keynes | HF (2010) | Dr Colin R. Masson | 1975 | Professor Gian Gabriele Ori | 1981 |
| Richard A. King | F (1986); EF (1996) | Ichiro Masuda | 1978 | Dr Arturo Ortiz-Tapia | 1995 |
| Dr Kerry Knight | 1994 | Dr Tiago Mata | 2000; F (2012) | Edward Oughton | 2010 |
| Dr Rika Kobayashi | 1988 | Professor Derek Matravers | | Elisabeth Overend | 1997 |
| Espen H. Koht | IT Manager | | 1987; Senior Member (2003) | | |
| Dr Ariane Kossack | 1999 | Dr Philip T. Matthews | 1995 | Dr Stefan Paetke | 1975 |
| Dr David P. Kreil | 1998; RF (2002) | Dr Wendy Matthews | 1987 | Roberto Paiva | 1999 |
| Dr Per Ola Kristensson | SF (2008) | Professor Ian McConnell | | Dr Ella Palmer | 2001 |
| Dr Torsten Krude | RF (1995); F (2000) | | 1967; F (2003); EF (2008) | Vittawat Panpanich | 2011 |
| Dr Steffen Krusch | 1995 | Professor Jacqueline McGlade | AF (1987) | Charles Dimitrios Papageorgiou | 2001 |
| Dr Angela Kühr | 2003 | Dr Ian McIvor | 1971 | Professor Patrick Parrinder | 1965 |
| | | Dr Brian McKeown | 1987 | Dr Barbara Sydney Parris | 1979 |
| Dr Noelle L'Hommedieu | 1979 | Dr Fiona McLaren | 1996 | Dr Isabelle Parsons | 2003 |
| Catarina Nunes Ladeira | 2003 | John McLeod | 1996 | Praveetha Patalay and Martin Patalay | 2009 |
| Guillaume Laganiere | 2012 | Professor Maureen McNeil | 1972 | The Hon. Dr Peter Patmore | 1976 |
| Professor Ron Laskey and Mrs Ann Laskey | | Richard D. McNeil | 1976 | Dr Karalyn Patterson | F (1991); EF (2009) |
| | F (1982); EF (2012) | Adam McWilliams | 2010 | Professor Georgia Pe-Piper | 1968 |
| Dr Nigel Law | 1974 | Dr Rita McWilliams Tullberg | 1966 | Montserrat Perera | 1973 |
| Dr Nicolas Le Roux | MiF (2008) | Smita Singhvi Mehta | 2005 | Robert J.D. Perera | 1989 |
| Dr Chang-Wook Lee | 2003 | Professor Hugh Mellor | F (1971) | Professor Richard Perham | HF (2004) |
| Dr Stuart J.W. Lee | 2005 | The Lady Margrit Methuen | 1986 | Dr Paul A. Perry | 1995 |
| Jintae Lee | 1981 | Dr Richard Meyrick | 1994 | Professor Dr N. and Dr B. Pfeiffer | 1984; 1984 |
| George Lenzi-Janhunen and | | Elaine Miller Bond | 1995 | Dr Helen A. Pfuhl | 1996 |
| Auli Lenzi-Janhunen | 1968; 1971 | Dr Tom Miller | 2008 | Dr Minh-Duy Phan | 2005 |
| Dr Bernard Leong | 1998 | Catherine Mills | 1970 | Dr Amyas Phillips and Dr Uma Phillips | |
| Jenny Frances Lesser | 2009 | Dr Victoria Mills | RF (2012) | | 2001; 2003 |
| Dr Rosemary Lethem | 1975 | Dr Celia P. Milstein | ES | Dr Clinton Pinto | 1993 |
| Aike Li | 2009 | Dr David Milway | 1982 | Dr David J.W. Piper | 1966 |
| Dao Tze Li | 1980 | Takayuki Miura | 2008 | Professor Andrew M. Pitts | F (1990) |
| Leo Liyuan Liao | 2002 | Dr Madan Babu Mohan | 2007 | Dr Derek Pocock | 1969 |
| Sisi Liao | 2008 | Aymeric Adam Monod-Gayraud | 2002 | Gudrun Politt | 1969 |
| Yuan Song Liao | 1991 | Dr Stephen H. Montgomery | 2007 | Dr Bojana Popovic | 2001 |
| Clara Lim-Tan | 1998 | Dr Melanie Moore | 1996 | Dr Andrew Porwancher | 2008 |
| Mengya Lin | 2011 | Dr Michal C. Moore | 1994 | Jennifer A. Power | 1989 |
| Roger Chin-Hung Lin | 1988 | Dr Terry Moore | 1985 | Dr Phillip Prager | 2003 |
| Dr Berend Lindner | 2001 | Hamid Moosavi | 2009 | Professor Herbert Prins | 1980 |
| Huanye Liu | 2009 | Azlan Morad | 1987 | Phillip Prodger | 1995 |
| Professor Sir Geoffrey Lloyd | | Dr David J. Morgan | 2002 | Ian D. Prosser | 1980 |
| | M (1989); HF (2000) | Dr Iain Morley | RF (2005) | Professor Gloria Pungetti | 1991 |
| Craig T. Lockwood | 2002 | Dr George W. Morris | 1985 | Veikko Punkka | 1989 |
| Professor Nicholas Long | AF (1992); F (1993) | Dr Michael Morrison | 1978 | Vinita Puri | 2013 |
| Dr Simon Loughe | 1981 | Dr Tina Mousley | 1977 | | |
| Dr Gordon Lovis | 1979 | Cherry Muijsson | 2011 | Shanshan Qiao | 2011 |
| Dr Jan Löwe | F (2012) | Dr Martyn Murray | 1982 | Bing Qu | 2004 |
| Jane Luard (née Darwin) | DF | Dr Sally Musson (née Boxell) | 1974 | Mary T. Quinn | 1991 |
| Dr L.H. Lumey | 1976 | | | | |
| Pierre A. Lurin | 1994 | Dr Ambili Nair | 1992 | Dragana Radojevic | 1998 |
| Dr Johan Lyhagen | VM (1999) | Professor Damian Nance | 1972 | Charlotte Rae | 2010 |
| | | Dr Amrita Narlikar | F (2008) | Paul Raekstad | 2012 |
| Professor David Macdonald | 1977 | Professor Manfred Nermuth | 1974 | Dr Cassandra D. Ragnauth | 2001 |
| Dr Andrew Mackintosh | 1978 | Dr André A. Neves | 1999 | Dr Gillian Ragsdale | 2001 |
| James P.R. MacLaren | 1985 | Dr Bruce A. Newton | F (1968); EF (1987) | John Rai | 2005 |

| | |
|---|---|
| Dr Sarah Ralph | 2000 |
| Jean Paul Raoul | 1972 |
| Dr Pamela Raspe | 1973 |
| The Hon. Robert A. Rayne | HF (2004) |
| Dr Michael L. Reakes | 1975 |
| Professor Martin Rees | HF (2004) |
| R.J.S. Reid | 1981 |
| Seth M. Reiss | 1983 |
| Dr Richard Rennie | 1978 |
| Isabel Cantidiano Ribeiro | 2005 |
| Dr Paul Ries | F (1973); EF (1999) |
| Barbara Susan Ritchie | 1982 |
| Frederic Rivain | 2000 |
| Dr David I. Robbins | 1995 |
| Dr Clementine H. Robert | 1969 |
| Yolanda Roberts (née Corley) | 1997 |
| Dr Douglas Robertson | 1996 |
| Dr Gordon Robin | FF |
| Ronald A. Robinette | 1976 |
| Dr Graham C. Robinson | 2005 |
| Graham Robinson | 1986 |
| Dr Arlindo José Rodrigues | 1989 |
| Dr Gerard Roe and Dr Helen McPartlan | |
| | 1987; 1988 |
| Dr Jaap Roording | 1994 |
| Dr Eckehard Rosenbaum | 1991 |
| Dáire Rowlands | 2012 |
| Mariya Rubanovskaya | 2003 |
| Kathleen Rudd Orndorff | 1993 |
| Dr Scott James Rufolo | 1998 |
| Dilbara Ryskeldinova and Ben Falcon | |
| | 2011; 2011 |
| | |
| Dr Aleksandr B. Sahakyan | 2008 |
| Dr Chris Sandbrook | F (2011) |
| Dr Daniel Sandler and Mrs Jennet Sandler | 1988 |
| Dr Sitthivet Santikarn | 1980 |
| Pawat Satayanurug | 2009 |
| Professor Kyozo Sato | 1973 |
| Andreas Sattler | 2003 |
| Dr Laurie Scandrett | 1979 |
| M.J.C. Scarborough | 2011 |
| Professor Frank Schaefer | 1998 |
| Dr Walter Scheidel | Finley F (1996) |
| Professor Brigitte Schludermann | 1970 |
| Alexander Schnebel | 2006 |
| Dr Eileen S. Scott | 1978 |
| Dr David Scotting | 1968 |
| Dr Jane M. Selby | 1977 |
| Professor Paul A. Selden | 1975 |
| Arnab Sengupta | 2002 |
| Sylvester Brian Setiadinata | 2011 |
| Professor Donna Seto-Young | 1976 |
| Dr David Shankland | 1986 |
| Professor William Shea | 1965 |
| Dr Jane Shen | 1986 |
| Dr David Shepherd and Dr Jennifer Shepherd | |
| | 2005; 2005 |

| | |
|---|---|
| Joseph Roy Sheppherd | 1982 |
| Dr Yibing Shi | 1988 |
| Wilbur Sim | 2011 |
| Professor Jefferson Cardia Simoes | 1984 |
| Dr Fiona Simpson | 1993 |
| Professor Sir Patrick Sissons | F (1988); EF (2012) |
| Michael David Sitch | 2002 |
| Dr Thomas H W Siu | 2004 |
| John Skinner | 1977 |
| Henrik Skovgaard-Petersen | 2010 |
| Dr Stephan Slingerland | 1993 |
| Dr P.M. Slocombe | 1973 |
| Dr Alex Smeets | 1985 |
| Dr Fiona Smith | 1995 |
| P.A.W. Smith | 1985 |
| Dr Ken Sneath | 2001 |
| Dr John Solly | 2002 |
| Dr Jamorn Somana | 2000 |
| Dr Joanne F. Sonin | 1995 |
| Somchai Sophastienphong | 1983 |
| Dr Graham Spinks | 1980 |
| Dr Klaus Staubermann | 1994 |
| Martin Stoeckinger | 2010 |
| Dr Cliff Studman and Mrs Irene Studman | 1971 |
| Dr Richard Suckling | 2008 |
| Professor Yasunori Sugimura | VM (2007) |
| Ma. Jacqueline P. Swann | 1996 |
| Walter Sweeney | 1982 |
| Dr Jan Szaif | 1990 |
| Dr Dénes Szűcs | F (2007) |
| | |
| Professor Dr Mayumi Taguchi | VM (1994) |
| Professor Toshiyuki Takamiya | 1975 |
| Dr Fui Ching Tan | 1997 |
| Bok Huat Tan | 1987 |
| Quentin Tannock | 2001 |
| Dr Grant Tapsell | RF (2003) |
| Baasanjav Terbish | 2008 |
| Dr Frederick Tey | 2005 |
| Professor Dame Jean Thomas | 1967; HF (2007) |
| Manjusha Thorpe | 2010 |
| Chris Todd | 1973 |
| Dr Jonathan Trevor and | |
| Dr Susannah Trevor | 2002; 2003 |
| Dr Patricia Tweeddale | 1969 |
| | |
| Professor Carlos Uribe-Celis | 1981 |
| | |
| Dr Giovanni Vaggi | 1971 |
| Richard van der Beek | 2011 |
| Dr Jenneke van der Wal | RF (2012) |
| Professor Richard C. Van Sluyters | 1972 |
| Betto van Waarden | 2011 |
| Paul A. Vayda | 2009 |
| Martha Viviana Vieyra | 1997 |
| Niel Viljoen | 1989 |
| Dr Maria J.P. Villalobos | 1988 |
| Professor Nigel Vincent | 1970 |

| | |
|---|---|
| Dr David Walker and Dr Carol Walker | |
| | 1972; 1973 |
| Dr Yalou Wang | 1997 |
| Dr David Ward | 2006 |
| Dr Kamol Wasapinyokul | 2006 |
| Dr Keith Watkins | 1978 |
| Dr Anthony J. Watson | 2007 |
| Professor William P. Weiner | 1984 |
| Dr Nick Weir | 1996 |
| Henry A. Wereko | 1989 |
| Dr Linda Wheeldon | 1985 |
| Dr Kathleen M. Wheeler | 1974; F (1990) |
| Dr Chester White | 1965; F (1969); EF (2001) |
| Dr David White | 1988 |
| Dr Roger Whitehead | F (1973); EF (2001) |
| Dr Terence J. Wieting | 1965 |
| Dr Mihirinie Wijayawardene | 1997 |
| Chris Wilde | 1976 |
| Dr Carol Anne Williams | 1969 |
| Dr Wyn Williams | 1982 |
| Nina Elspeth Williams (née Dick) | 1989 |
| Avril Williams | Housekeeping Staff |
| Susan Williams (née Jennings) | 1993 |
| Professor Michael Wilson | 1980 |
| Alison M. Wilson (née Gomm) | 1969 |
| Dr David Wiltshire | 1983 |
| Diana Wingfield (née Harris) | 1969 |
| Dr Kin Hong Wong | 1982 |
| Oi Hoong Wong | 1975 |
| Gordon Chung-Leung Wong | 1991 |
| Professor Patricia Woo | 1977 |
| Helen Wood | 1970 |
| Professor John Wood | 1971 |
| Dr Nigel I. Wood | 1995 |
| Professor Jamie Woodward | 1986 |
| Dr Chris Wright | 2006 |
| Carlos Graham Wright | 1993 |
| Dr Edward Wright | 1980 |
| Dr Liang-Ta Wu | 2008 |
| Dr Karen Wynter (née Newstead) | 1991 |
| Dr Wilhelmus Wytenburg | 1987 |
| | |
| Doron Yacobi | 2004 |
| Dr Pei-Jung Yang | 2006 |
| Dr Ye Yeo | 2000 |
| Seong Teik Yeoh | 2000 |
| Huang Yiyan (Vicky) | 2002 |
| Dr Abe Yoffe | FF |
| Petra Young (née Kobertova) | 1992 |
| Shu Yu | 2008 |
| Eiichi Yubune | 1998 |
| Dr Julia Zaccai | 2002 |
| Dr Steve Zan | 1987 |
| Sarit Avny Zerubavel | 2008 |
| Dr Yun-Ling Zheng | 1990 |
| Dr Rue W. Ziegler | 1992 |

# INDEX

Page references in *italics* indicate captions for images; those in **bold** denote authorship.